THE BOOK OF
FIVE CYPHERS

CORY HOWELL

Second Edition – April 2016

The Book of Five Cyphers, written by Cory Howell

Cover and Book Layout by Tadashi Tomomune

Publishing Coordinated by Lillygol Sedaghat

Calligraphy by Tomomi Matsumura

Edited by Susan Howell and Lillygol Sedaghat

Printed in the United States of America

ISBN: 978-0-692-67180-1

CONTENTS

ACKNOWLEDGEMENTS

Thank you Tadashi Tomomune for your tireless efforts in designing the book cover, and putting this book together. Thank you as well for being the first person to read this book in its entirety and offering your amazing skills. This project would have gotten nowhere without you.

Thank you to Tomomi Matsumura for capturing traditional Japanese sentiments with your elegant calligraphy. Our love and appreciation for you and Tadashi is real.

A special thanks and shout out to all the community members that contributed to this book! Thank you to RawSkeleton for always being an inspiration to me and sharing your insight. Thank you to Whacko for beautifully expressing your journey in such a wonderful way. Thank you to Eddie Styles for being a mentor to me and continuing to share your incredible knowledge with the community. Thank you to Sumo for sharing your love and hunger for the dance and for always pushing the scene to be better. Thank you to Ark for sharing your insights on your crew and your journey, and always killing it wherever you go. Thank you to M-Pact for being a shining light to the community and an ambassador for bboys and bgirls everywhere. Thank you to Francis for showing us we can overcome any obstacle. Thank you to Ken Masters for helping build the community and next gen, and for being my eternal rival.

Thank you as well to each one of my crew members for walking the Path with me. You're my brothers and I love you all dearly. Special shout out to Rey-S for building our website, Pacifico for shooting our photos, and Neat-O Suave for hosting the Jam of Five Cyphers.

Thank you to my mom for staying up late nights to edit this book with me. You're awesome mom!

Finally, thank you to my partner Lilly Sedaghat for pushing me to get this project off the ground. Without you, this book would still be a file on my Google Drive. I love you.

P R E F A C E

Warriors and generals have been thinking and writing about battle for thousands of years. *The Art of War* is a text ascribed to Sun Tzu, a high ranking Chinese general, that has become the inspiration for countless people who think about and engage in battle. Published in 514 BCE, it became the quintessential text for strategists thereafter and has influenced not just the world's militaries, but artists, businessmen, scholars—anyone who knows they'll interact with others.

More than two thousand years later, Japan saw the rise of Miyamoto Musashi, one of the most prolific samurai in Japanese history. Musashi was heavily influenced by Sun Tzu, but also took his own Path in search of the Way. He wrote his findings in *The Book of Five Rings* in 1645 CE.

In recent years, Alien Ness wrote *The Art of Battle* to give bboys the decisive manual to prepare for and win judged battles. His book was written in the style of Sun Tzu's *The Art of War* and draws many parallels to Sun Tzu's work, while spelling out lessons specifically for bboys.

In writing *The Book of Five Cyphers*, I thought to add to this discourse. In the way that Musashi came after Sun Tzu, I'm writing after Ness' *The Art of Battle*. Much like Ness modeled his book on *The Art of War*, I'm borrowing both Musashi's structure and form, and using his didactic voice in many of my passages. Similar to the way Musashi meant to build on Sun Tzu, I'm writing about more than just the judged bboy/bgirl battle, and my hope is that by reading this you can grow as a competitive bboy or bgirl, as a dancer, and as a person.

UNDERSTANDING MY INTENTION

In writing *The Book of Five Cyphers,* I'm not trying to create an encyclopedia of bboying/bgirling. Most of the examples I give should be understood as embodying the spirit of the concept I'm talking about.

Nothing in the pages that follow is meant to be comprehensive. You will find that lists I give are incomplete, and if you think hard enough about what I say, I'm sure you'll be able to find exceptions.

If you focus on the trees though, you'll miss the forest. Please understand that in writing *The Book of Five Cyphers,* my intention is to give you focus and direction to grow as a dancer and person—it was never meant to be all encompassing. The purpose of this book is to get you to think about bboying/bgirling and try new concepts and new ways of thought and movement.

A NOTE ABOUT TERMS IN
THE BOOK OF FIVE CYPHERS

I use different terminology in *The Book of Five Cyphers* and sometimes generalize as a result. None of this is meant to offend or be inaccurate—please understand the spirit of what I am saying. The most obvious terms that I sometimes use in a general sense I'd like to address here:

Breaking – Another generic term for bboying and bgirling. Breaking, however, tends to have the negative connotation of "breakdancing," and indicates the moves themselves, not the culture or mindset. When I do use it, please understand that I simply mean to refer to the movements of the dance in general.

Sets – I often use this to mean a "round," "go down," or "run." Know that I generally disagree with the thought of using completely premeditated sets, and simply use this to mean the package of moves that you use when on the floor.

THE BOOK OF EARTH

THE BOOK OF EARTH

This is about the more practical aspects of the dance, which includes the state of things as I see them at the moment, and ideas about how to practice. This will help you execute and build your own style to obtain a greater understanding of dancing as a whole.

In reading the Earth Book, you should not expect to use all of the things presented here—rather, you should keep an open mind and try to understand as much as possible, know that I have missed things, and apply what you find useful. While you should only apply what speaks to you, understanding that there are other concepts out there is one of the keys to this section.

THE "INTANGIBLE" STUFF ABOUT BBOYING

WHERE WE'RE AT NOW

I'm assuming that if you're reading this, you have at least some knowledge about Hip Hop, the Elements, and general history. If not, I encourage you to learn more about it—to understand where you're at it helps to know where you've been. If you haven't seen them already, start by watching The Freshest Kids, Style Wars, and Wild Style.

I'm writing this at a time of great tension in bboying/bgirling. In retrospect, there has always been great tension in the dance. Ken Swift talked about bboying/bgirling rising out of a landscape with very few social resources—when things are so negative that you get used to difficulty in your day to day life, you latch onto something positive when you find it.

The early 80's brought bboying/bgirling into popular culture through film and TV, and there was a great tension between what we now know as bboys/bgirls, and what we would distinguish as breakdancers. In the mid 80's, we saw breaking fall out as a fad, and go underground where it developed in the US and internationally. The 90's saw bboying/bgirling struggle to understand itself as a dance and culture and find its place in relation to Hip Hop.

At the moment, we're seeing a tension among many different schools of thought in the dance. Perhaps the two largest are those that maintain that the dance should stay in the streets, battles should be "raw," and bboying/bgirling should always be a counter-culture. The other primary school of thought asserts that we as dancers should be professionals, be able to make a living dancing, and hold ourselves to the same standards as professional athletes.

Know that as the author of this book, I am trying to maintain a sense of neutrality in terms of the politics of the dance, and want to discuss your development as a dancer and artist. Whatever position you take on the direction of bboying/bgirling, it is important that you educate yourself—never stop learning about the dance and your place in the world. Keep an open mind, and by that I mean respect the opinions of others—when you're evaluating the merit of any opinion or argument start from a place of neutrality. Do not initially assume something is right or wrong, and start from a neutral place and evaluate for yourself. Always continue learning.

COMMERCIAL THINGS
(PEOPLE WHO SELL THEIR SWORD)

Know that bboying/bgirling is something that can potentially make money—although making bboying/bgirling profitable can be extremely difficult. When determining if it is worth it, you must consider if "selling your sword" to your potential client or audience is proper.

Selling your sword to share your knowledge may be a worthwhile endeavor. You must determine if selling your sword for an audience of lay-people (non-dancers) is worth it for you. Those that only learn to do windmills or handhops to impress people in a club are not dancers or artists—they are people that know how to do windmills or handhops.

Roxrite is one of the best bboys in the world and makes a living as an artist for Red Bull. When I asked him how he felt about those that called dancing for Red Bull a "commercial" endeavor, he told me that the Red Bull coordinators have never once asked him to change the way he dances—Roxrite has maintained his artistic integrity while making a living through the dance.

If you wish to make bboying profitable, consider your integrity as a dancer and a person.

WHAT IS HEIHO (兵法)?

Put simply, Heiho is the Art of War. Heiho is a term that I've borrowed from Miyamoto Musashi when he discusses his specific way of thinking about and engaging in battle. It encompasses not just ideas about fighting, but ways of thinking about strategy and war, and is a general compass for life.

5

Know that my Heiho is not one that is simply about dancing, but is the Path of the student as well. You must walk the Path of both Warrior and Scholar. You must practice diligently and always study.

THE PATH (道) OF HEIHO

The Path is a metaphor that I often use when talking about our careers as dancers or more generally, our lives. The character for path, street, or way (道) is one used in Chinese and Japanese to denote a larger idea of traveling—it is the same character used in the names of many martial arts, and is used for the word "Tao" (as in "Taoism" or "Daoism").

I capitalize the word "Path" to indicate the metaphorical Path, not a literal one. Much like an actual street has twists, turns, potholes, and does not always run perfectly straight, you must understand that your Path will take you in many different directions, and you often can't see around the next corner. Practicing and studying at all times can help you walk the Path. Your Path should not come to an end by winning a jam, getting a gig, or even suffering an injury. You must understand this fully.

WHY DID I WRITE
THE BOOK OF FIVE CYPHERS?

I do not have all the answers. There are gaps in my abilities. I have, however, been able to compete with strong dancers because I do my best to understand the dance. I've noticed that there are many dancers with great physical or creative potential, but who lack direction and resources to improve their mental game. I'm writing this book to give those bboys/bgirls direction—this is not just to teach dancers specific skills, but to give them a foundation of knowledge to continue educating themselves about dancing, and hopefully to apply that knowledge to their lives. We should constantly be striving to better ourselves and always learn.

ABOUT BBOYING/BGIRLING—THE BASICS

THE PRIMARY WEAPONS OF BBOYING/BGIRLING

Within bboying/bgirling there are four primary weapons. I won't dwell on them too much, but understand that these exist as four specific aspects of the dance.

Toprock—Dancing on your feet, prior to hitting the floor. Different schools of thought exist regarding whether toprock is a dance in and of itself, or whether toprock denotes that moves on the floor must follow.

Footwork/Floorwork—Dancing on the floor, including steps, patterns, flows, backrocks, threads on the floor, and the like.

Powermoves—Any dynamic spinning move such as windmills, swipes, flares, airflares, 90's, halos, floats, and the like.

Freezes—Any move that stops your motion. Freezes can be anything from a standing pose to airchairs, as well as moves like hollowbacks, inverts, and head freezes.

*Some bboys/bgirls will argue that there are five primary components of bboying, separating powermoves into "spins" and "moves in the air" (flares, airflares, flips). I've kept it at four components because this keeps them understandable, and if we identify too many components, we could find many exceptions (we'd then have to account for low spins, high spins, and air moves, blow ups, stacks, and a number of others. We could also separate footwork and floorwork and create even more distinctions from there). In leaving out "moves in the air," I'm not suggesting that these moves are "not bboying or bgirling."

USING WEAPONS TO YOUR ADVANTAGE

Many bboys/bgirls specialize in one or two weapons. In my school of Heiho, you should study all weapons, and be able to use them effectively if you need to. If you would then like to remove these things from your vocabulary and specialize in using a specific weapon, feel free to do so—however, this should only be done after you understand the nuances of the other weapons.

You should also know how to use your weapons effectively, how to combine them, and how to use them properly against your opponent. I'll go over the specifics of how to use your weapons in later sections.

THE PRIMARY STYLES IN BBOYING/BGIRLING

While there are many different styles in bboying/bgirling, I'm cataloging a few of them for you to consider. Keep in mind that you should not limit yourself to any one of these styles—calling yourself a "Style Head" or a "Power Head" only serves to limit yourself. Rather, you should understand that these schools of thought exist, and if you decide that you would like to specialize in anything in particular, do so with intention.

Also understand that while the internet has made us all closer together, there still tend to be many regional styles—even within the United States, dancers from different cities often have unique form and vibes.

Traditional "Style" – Dancers who use a traditional New York style form. Dancers to look at would be Rock Steady Crew and Dynamic Rockers. Bboys like Ken Swift have style that still holds up today— anyone using the form that existed even as far back as the 1970's could be said to have a traditional style.

Crews like Rock So Fresh have studied and paid attention to the traditional style and mentality, but add their own flavor to distinguish themselves—if you choose to dance in a traditional style, know that you don't have to limit yourself.

Brand New Old School – I've borrowed the saying "Brand New Old School" from Boogie Brats and Rivers Crew. These are dancers that use a form similar to the traditional New York style, but tend to add more technical concepts, and possibly power and blow ups. Look at bboys/bgirls like Rivers Crew, Flo Mo, and the newer (and international) members of Mighty Zulu Kings for a sense of what this looks like. Much like the Traditional Style, you don't have to limit yourself because of the form you like.

New School – New School Bboys/Bgirls are those that use a relatively standard form, but tend to focus more on dynamics and trending moves. Crews like Drifterz Crew, Jinjo, Foundnation, Momentum Crew, The Ruggeds, Top 9, Predatorz, Knuckleheads (CA and Zoo), and Skill Methods would be good examples of these types of dancers. These styles tend to be the most prevalent at the moment, and are usually the most effective for doing well at a jam. Beware of falling into the trap of dancing too much like others.

Power – These are bboys/bgirls that push the limits of powermoves. Bboys like The End, Bruce Lee, Kaku, Yosshi, Blonde, Blue, Ryuji, Lil Kev, Tawfiq, Lil G, Kill, and Lil Ceng are excellent examples of what this style looks like when excecuted well. If you choose to employ a power-style, know you may have to overcome issues of well-roundedness and battle stamina (especially if you are interested in 1v1 formats). Also know that you can overcome this with training. Power-style bboys/bgirls tend to be extremely effective in crew battles.

Spins – Some bboys/bgirls specialize specifically in spins. While rotations for powermoves like windmills and flares can be categorized by rotating around your body (generally you'll be facing the floor during the "back" of the move, and face up during the "front" of the move), some powermoves maintain a static rotating position. These spins include 90's, 2000's, headspins, backspins, and shoulderspins. Spin bboys to note are Blast, Lazer, and Aichi. This style tends to work well for shows and crew battles, but can be limiting in other situations.

Tricks/Blow Ups – Bboys that specialize in tricks and blow ups take freezes, freeze stacks, and freeze combinations to high levels—they often use them in combination with power moves and flips. Some bboys with strong blow ups include Ryoma, Juju, Lil Clash, Luan, and Lil Sin.

Taower, Tawfiq, and Kill are examples of bboys that have powerful blow ups and mix them with a powermove style. These bboys can have huge potential for exciting crowds and smoking their opponents. Know that if you employ this style, you may have to overcome issues of repeating in later rounds—know that you can work around these limitations by creating variety in your moves.

Strong Style – These bboys/bgirls use many static moves and freezes—often in combination with other styles. They often use slow motion, one armed balance, and planches as a show of strength. Good bboys to see as an example of strong style are Kujo, Pop, and Jibaku. If you chose to employ strong style, learn to pace your sets and come to a strong finish. Try to develop moves that have the same "punch," that a dynamic powermove or trick may have.

Abstract – Abstract bboys/bgirls utilize a style that focuses on creativity, flexibility, and expression. These bboys/bgirls usually focus on unique bodily combinations, threads, and freezes when they dance. Examples of abstract bboys include Nick Abatt from Artistics Tribe/Stylements, Freakazoid and Raw Skeleton from The Freak Show, Josh from Circus Runaways, as well as Insane Prototypes, and Illusion of Exist. Know that this style is extremely powerful, but you may have to overcome some bias from those who might not understand your movement. You can overcome this through persistance, good packaging, and strong battle presence.

Post-Modern – Post-Modern bboys/bgirls push the limits of what it means to dance or bboy. These dancers strive to expand what it means to bboy and usually use creative movements to manifest this. The style is often a response to or a rejection of traditional styles of bboying/bgirling or art and highly values self-expression, musicality, and experimental form. This is one of the riskier styles of dance and often doesn't get classified as "bboying/bgirling." If you're interested, you could look up Post-Modern artistic movements of the 20th century to understand more about the conceptual framework regarding the thought process behind this. Good bboys to find as examples of Post-Modern bboys are Katsu, Quick, Prince, and Non-Man from Ichigeki, Nobunaga and Detail (Rowdy) from EXG, Morning of Owl, and Illusion of Exist.

PRACTICING

THE PRACTICAL STUFF

The myriad pieces that come together to form a practice are all important—you must control as many as possible to create the type of practice that will fulfill what you need. Know that energy is one of the most important factors to consider when you're practicing—energy dominates and will qualify your entire practice. You must control the energy as much as possible to have an effective practice.

Recognize that if you don't practice hard or well, you're being dishonest to yourself and robbing yourself of something important. Respect yourself enough to practice effectively. Being dishonest with yourself is bad discipline.

The Space – Consider where you are practicing. Is it a gym with high ceilings or a garage with a low ceiling? Is it hot or cold? Is it drafty or outdoors? The energy from each of these spaces will be quite different—while no space is superior to another, you must find your personal preference, and maximize the efficiency of your practice. Avoiding cold spaces makes for longer practices. High ceilings and open spaces may cause you to get tired faster because your energy will disperse faster. Although, when training for an event you know will be cold or in an open space, it can be beneficial to practice in these environments.

The Floor – Consider the floor you are practicing on. Is it carpet, concrete, linoleum, wood or marley dance floor, spring floor, trampoline, grass, sand, or dirt? As with the space, different floors will allow you to do different things, and they will give and get different things. Carpet tends to maintain heat, and thus keep energy in a practice. Concrete tends to be harder on your body but forces you to be clean in your movements. Spring floor and trampolines can allow you to try risky moves. Sand and grass can bring out a more natural feel in your practice.

Try to be intentional about the ground that you'd like to practice on, and focus on sustainability. It is good to occasionally practice on a difficult floor—if you can practice in a "worst case scenario," you can dance anywhere. Usually, however, those situations aren't sustainable and your practice should allow you to continue a long-term schedule in a healthy manner.

The People – More important than the space or the floor are the people you practice with. A crew should be a group of individuals who support one another, reminiscent of a family. While floors and spaces reflect, retain, and take your energy, people have the ability to both give and take energy. Be sure to practice with supportive people who are invested in your growth and will be positive. Avoid practicing with negative people or those that drain your energy.

Understand that you will inherently start dancing like the people around you, and they will start dancing like you. For this reason, try to practice with people at or above your skill level. If it is unavoidable and you have to practice with others not at your level, understand this principle and be intentional about how to progress in the midst of this.

Also understand that practices with small numbers or big groups will yield different energies and different practices. While small practices tend to have less potential energy, they can be highly energetic and productive if you're sharing energy. Although large practices can have more potential energy, if you're with a group of people that drain energy, it could potentially be less productive.

Note as well that there are different types of practices that you can go to—you can't control who goes to a community open floor and you may be subject to negative energy in such an environment.

At a closed crew practice, though, you are much more likely to vibe well and get positive energy from those you are dancing with. Understand that these different spaces exist, and work to modify your expectations and practice depending on where you go and what you are trying to achieve.

The Music – The music is one of the most (arguably the single most) important parts of your practice. While it is imperative that you listen to popular breaks in preparation for competition, you must also understand that practicing to different types of music will yield different results; put simply, you will dance differently to different songs.

It is important to practice to both high tempo and low tempo music—you may get low or high BPM (beats per minute) songs at a jam, and it is important to be able to dance to any of them. Practicing routines to songs of different tempos will also help your squad's chemistry.

You must also occasionally practice to music or songs that you dislike. While this should not be a part of your typical routine, if there is a popular song that you fear getting in a battle, you should figure out a way to dance to it. While the music at a jam is not a variable you can control, by preparing in a safe environment, you can be ready when you get to a jam.

Music also plays an important part in your lab sessions. Keep in mind that the music that you lab to will change the way you dance and spark different creative parts of your brain. Do all things with intention.

ON NOT BECOMING DEPENDENT ON OTHERS AT PRACTICE

It helps to have friends and crewmembers with you at practice, but it becomes detrimental to rely too much on others. There may be times you show up and no one is there (or no one from your crew), or people are tired and unmotivated. While working with the energy of others can help with execution, building relationships and chemistry, and generally vibing, you must learn how to have a constructive practice with only your own energy.

Sometimes when I arrive to practice ten or fifteen minutes late, no one is warmed up—people at my practice space tend to wait for me to start. Rather than reliance on others, you must cultivate your self-discipline to have a constructive practice no matter what. Allow yourself to practice differently with and without the energy of others. Generally, it should be irrelevant if you are the only person at practice, or if there are 40 people—you must develop the ability to be constructive in either environment.

ON PRACTICING MOVES

Practicing "moves" is an important part of building your repertoire as a dancer. While it is important to always work on your form and make your style natural, it is also important to constantly be developing new moves. I'm not advocating for always getting new blow ups or power moves; rather, you should always be expanding your vocabulary in all aspects of the dance (blowups and power are fine if that is what you want). Neat-o Suave of Uncomfortably Fresh suggested that for new moves, you should employ LAPSI:

Labbing: Developing ideas. When you're working in the lab, you should be by yourself, at most with a few crew members. You should be in a space where you can focus within yourself to think, maintain energy for an extended period of time, and use music that speaks to your creative and expressive self. Take the time to try things out—don't worry about looking silly. Move from within yourself.

Applying: When you feel you've developed a usable idea, make it applicable in your rounds. Film yourself doing the move, practice it in context, put other moves around it, and try it to music. Try variations of the move and see if there are tweaks you can do to make it better. Get feedback from your crew.

Perfecting: You should get to the point where you can use your new move at any time, in any context. This is when you start to develop muscle memory for the move. Try using it in different places. Do it in front of people. Start practicing the move at session. If the move is one that you have any reservations about, you should now get it to the point where you can hit it at any time.

Second Nature: Although "perfecting" the move means working out the technical aspects of doing it properly, you should now make the move organic to your very being. There is both a mental and physiological difference to doing moves at a practice and at a battle—you must get your moves to the point where you can execute without thinking about them. When you're in a situation (battle) where you can't control all the variables, your moves must be under your control.

Influence: After you've been able to use the moves in a battle, take some time to honestly evaluate. How did the crowd react? How did it feel doing the move in context? Was there anything you would change? This is also the time to get further feedback from your crew and to begin tweaking and expanding the move if need be.

Consider periodically recycling your moves by tweaking them and doing them in slightly different contexts so that they don't get stale. Try to avoid doing entirely premeditated sets. I'll talk more about set construction later on in the Earth Book.

ON LABBING

Hip Hop heads have long used the term "labbing" to denote the process of developing new ideas. The term comes from the idea of a scientist developing new theories in the laboratory. The analogy doesn't stop there, and when you're spending time in the lab you should take on the attitude of a scientist at work. When I say this, I don't necessarily mean that you should be bland and sterile about the process, but rather, be okay with failure. Scientists often run hundreds, sometimes thousands of experiments before developing a usable idea. In the same way, we as dancers should not be afraid of failing in the lab, but should be persistent. If something doesn't work, try it in a different way or try something else.

It is important to spend time in the lab as well as "session" (practicing things in context). Each type of practice accomplishes different things—you cannot be a complete bboy/bgirl without doing both.

How much time you spend in the lab depends on your desire to create new moves. However you decide to approach it, create a space and atmosphere where you can be honest with yourself and play around—have fun and try whatever comes to mind.

Try things both that make sense and things that don't seem to flow together. When I asked M-Pact of Underground Flow and Shyism of Calamities what their creative process was, they mentioned that they work to take two seemingly unrelated moves that don't flow together, and figure out a way to properly transition between them. M-Pact discusses more about developing flow and ideas in the Book of Emptiness. Try things out and constantly be practicing.

ON PRACTICING STYLE/FLOW

While labbing and perfecting your move repertoire is important, you should also work on your style and flow.

By "style," I mean your actual form and the narrative that you tell through your dance. It is important to understand how you look when you dance—bboys/bgirls often say that you should be able to dance "raw," and that you don't need a mirror but should just feel it. While you can't physically see yourself dancing in a cypher or battle, it is important to take your practice time to perfect your form. Do toprock, power, and freezes in front of the mirror. Record and watch yourself. Make small tweaks to your angles and adjust your approach to certain moves. Only by building your form through practice will you be able to express yourself properly when you want to "feel it" at a jam or when bugging out with others.

By "flow" I mean your ability to transition properly between moves and piece your moves together. Similar to your style, you must meticulously build your repertoire and be intentional about how you do so. Become comfortable with your moves, so that when you do them in context, they will come out properly. Only through practice from the ground up will you be able to properly develop your flow and feel comfortable using it in the cypher or in a battle.

ON PRACTICING FOR BATTLE

I reject the idea of "practicing for a jam." In my school of Heiho, you should always be ready to battle. Jams and competitions themselves are but a step on the Path—you should always seek to improve as much as possible at all times. If you feel you need to practice more for a jam specifically, you should have been practicing harder from the beginning of your Path.

With that said, there are certain things you can do to prepare yourself for a battle in your day to day practice. You should always be practicing for battles, so that when the time does arrive, it will be second nature to you. Generally, the following things will help prepare you physically and mentally for a battle:

Going Rounds – The best way to practice for a battle is to actually practice battling—while this seems obvious, it must be stated. Go rounds with someone at every practice. Ideally, you want to go rounds with someone at your level or above. Even when people claim to want to "go easy" in rounds, the minute they're thrown into a battle situation and feel like they're losing, they'll go all out. Getting used to battling against someone will help you with the feeling of needing to execute in context.

Do Full Go-Downs – Even when you're practicing by yourself, work on doing full go-downs. Practicing individual moves is very important when working to develop a new skill (a new powermove, new freeze, or new transition), but you should take some time every practice to do full go-downs. Not only will this help you prep physically, but you'll mentally become used to the idea of needing to package things.

Cardio – Going rounds and doing full go-downs are excellent ways to condition your body and lungs. Additionally, you should do a few cardio intensive exercises. My crewmate Rox-it developed the drill of doing moves "30 seconds on, 30 seconds off" to simulate doing rounds. For instance, with a friend or crewmember, take turns doing 30 second runs of footwork—don't leave the floor unoccupied. As soon as one person's 30 seconds are up, the other should be on the floor—and back and forth. You should do six total rounds each and the drill will take six minutes. Done properly, this is an extremely difficult drill that will greatly enhance your endurance.

Practice in Front of People – One of the "variables" (I will talk more about this in the Fire Book) that you have to contend with in battles is the crowd. While you can't bring 50 or 300 people to every single practice with you to get used to dancing in front of a moving, breathing crowd, there are some ways to get used to this. Go to open floor sessions and go rounds with a crewmember— everyone there will instinctively stop to watch when they see someone "battling." Another option is to go to a public space with lots of people and practice. Both of these may feel uncomfortable at first, but they'll get you used to practicing in front of people, and you'll feel more comfortable during a battle.

LEARN TO FREESTYLE

Being able to freestyle is an important part of bboying/bgirling in my school of Heiho. When you are a bboy/bgirl who does planned sets, you become inflexible. Not only do you become predictable, but you lose the ability to properly articulate the music. I must say that there is a misconception about "freestyling." Most people feel that freestyling means making up moves on the spot—while this is an option for some (and one definition of freestyle), it doesn't always look good for others. When I say you are freestyling, this means that you are putting your moves together in a free and unique way to the music and the context around you—generally, though, you are using the weapons that you already have under control, just in a unique composition.

You must develop moves that you can do at any point in your set, and you must develop a group of moves that you can use to articulate different sounds in songs. I'll talk more about working with music in the Water Book, but you must develop the ability to execute to any different song. Become unpredictable. You must practice this diligently.

LEARN TO DANCE ON BEAT

Much like learning to freestyle, you must learn to rock different parts of the beat. The combination of physical prowess and artistry is the apex of bboying/bgirling. Rather than simply using your moves mindlessly, you must learn to do things on beat. Practice to different kinds of music, and practice using each one of your weapons (tops, footwork, power, freezes) to different songs. Become comfortable with articulating the music with each one of your weapons. You should always be practicing this.

ON BEING POSITIVE

I can't stress enough how important it is to be positive. You must remain positive at all times. If ever you have a negative thought, delete it from your mind and move on. This is one of the keys to staying on the Path—by staying positive you can remain dancing and stay constructive for a long time.

Before I go on, I must distinguish between being positive and being realistic—you must also be realistic. The discussion of being "realistic" has to do with the practical; don't try to learn airchairs if your arm is broken; if you've pulled a muscle, let it rest; don't try to learn flips if you haven't built up to them. Additionally, understand that you may have moments when you're disappointed in yourself, your performance, or your progress. Let the moment happen but don't dwell on it—move on.

Positivity should lead you through your entire dance career. Give encouragement to others at practice—smiling, giving props, and being positive can go a long way. Never insult your crewmembers, friends, or even your enemies at practice. If someone needs feedback, pay attention to how you articulate yourself—don't say "that sucked" or "that was wack." Instead, offer constructive advice. Steer them in the right direction.

By coming from a place of negativity, you will ultimately hurt yourself in your career. If you maintain positivity, you'll not only have better practices and do better at jams, you'll also build powerful allies.

Keep in mind this is something that you must continually do. Please don't read this, go to a jam, try have a positive attitude for an hour and expect yourself to win—this is something you must cultivate over time and consistently develop.

Be positive, be realistic about your shortcomings, and be solution oriented. You must understand this fully.

OVERCOMING NERVOUSNESS

Nervousness is a reality that many dancers face. Gaining experience, dancing for extended periods of time, and getting used to the feeling of performing and battling in front of people will help you gain confidence. Even so, you may still be subject to nervousness. That is okay and it is natural. Here are a couple things to keep in mind when considering your state of nervousness:

You May Always Be Nervous – You might always be nervous when dancing and that's okay. The important thing is to control your nervousness. Nervousness is a combination of mental and physical reactions to stress—knowing that it is happening to you can actually help you overcome it. You'll expend huge amounts of energy by being nervous, so recognize when it is happening to you—when you hit that point of recognition, you can actually be more in control. Don't be reactive, know your situation, and make intentional moves from there.

Take Your Time – When dancers are nervous, they tend to rush their moves and sets to try to get out of the circle quickly. When you recognize your nervousness, make an intentional effort to take

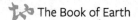

your time and go at your own pace. You'll be surprised how much this helps.

Breathe – Much like taking your time, taking deep breaths before entering a circle or battle can help you. Again, start with a point of recognition: "I'm nervous, but that's okay." Then calm yourself down with deep breaths. You'll feel more in control of yourself and your dance.

Recognize that the Crowd and Judges Want You to Kill It – No spectator at a jam ever wants you to do poorly—they want to see cool moves and good dancing. The energy of 200 or 300 people is like that of a rushing river—if you try to move against the energy of the crowd, you will without a doubt fail. If, however, you recognize that everyone wants you to do well and you flow with the current, you can benefit immensely. Use their energy to your advantage and gain confidence in knowing that people want you to dance well.

The only person or people that may want you to do poorly are your opponents. As I said above though, if you move with the energy of the crowd and judges, you can overcome any nervousness knowing they are on your side. Even so, sometimes your opponents will want you to do well because they'll want a challenge or a hype battle. Know this and do your best.

ON GETTING INJURED

Injuries are inevitable in bboying/bgirling. Whether an injury that happens results from a wet floor, someone getting in your way, a distraction, a bad decision, or your own lack of focus, you should know that eventually you may get injured. You must control what you can and be patient with yourself. I thought to include this in the Water Book, but because it deals with the body, it is included in the Earth Book. Know that this section has Water elements to it—you must understand the full implications of this.

Be Selective About Your Practice Space/Partners – As I mentioned earlier in the Earth Book, be selective about who you practice with. Do not tolerate people who will distract you from practice, or who try to intentionally break your concentration or get in your way when you're working on a dangerous move. True, you should be able to weather distraction in a battle, but only after your moves are second nature.

Practice Smart, Not Hard – Of course you should practice hard. Push yourself to the limits! Do however, be smart about pain. Learn to distinguish between muscle fatigue or "the burn," and your joints, tendons, or bones hurting. You should push your muscles to make them stronger. The moment you feel your joints, tendons, or bones hurting, ease back. Practicing on an injury will detract from your progress in the long run.

Take Proper Rest – Resting is part of training. Do not be the type of person who prides themselves on being able to forego rest—this is foolish. You should take care of yourself and rest appropriately. Lack of sleep will hurt your performance. Especially the night before a battle, get proper rest and don't take alcohol. If you must drink, do so after the battle.

Likewise, if you're injured, do not practice on your injury. You'll feel better before you are better. Be smart about it.

Work Around Your Injuries – I fully understand that you'll want to dance and practice when you're hurt. If this is the case and you want to maintain certain aspects of your dance, work around your injury. If your wrist is hurt, work on toprock, one handed footwork and moves on one arm. If your leg is hurt, work on strong style moves. Learning work-arounds can open up doors for your dance.

Rehab Yourself (Minor Injuries) – Athletes who hurt themselves often have physical therapy to strengthen the injured part of their body. Develop safe training methods to strengthen that part of your body so you can come back stronger and prevent injury later. I am not a doctor, so I cannot offer medical advice, nor do I intend to. However, much in the same way that you strengthen your moves before you can try harder ones, you can strengthen your body to help prevent injuries as much as possible.

You should always stretch and take care of yourself. While injuries are unavoidable, you can deal with them in a smart, safe, and mature way. As Denzel Washington said in Training Day, "This shit's chess, it ain't checkers." Think of the long-term. You may have to give up practice for several days, but you may save yourself an injury that could hurt your dance for months or years.

If you seriously hurt yourself—anything above minor tweaks, cuts, bruises, sprains, and that sort of thing, be mature about it and consult a medical professional.

HOW TO BUILD YOUR BBOYING/BGIRLING: PRAGMATICS ABOUT YOUR DANCE

This section is about the core curriculum of Five Cyphers 101. It will discuss how to actually build your sets, what pieces you will need to master to make your sets stronger, and how to practice them. If you can master what comes in this section, you will become a bboy/bgirl that is "difficult to beat." From that point, you must continue learning and practicing to take yourself to a higher level.

ABOUT CONSTRUCTING YOUR SETS

Set construction or "packaging" is one of the most important things you must initially master when thinking about your bboying/bgirling. I often see bboys/bgirls that throw lots of powerful moves haphazardly in a set, get up and reset with toprock several times, or walk out of a set after throwing crazy moves and wonder why they lost.

By packaging your moves well, you can not only increase the effectiveness of the moves that you do use, but convince those around you that you are airtight.

Poe One taught me the idea of set construction and related it to a narrative—your go-down must be like a story: there is a coherent beginning, middle, and end. You shouldn't have a beginning in the middle of your story, and likewise, the ending shouldn't come first. Of course, like with many movies and stories, you can play with narrative structure (we've all seen the types of movie where the end comes first and then you figure out what happened), but the key here is intention. You must tell your story on purpose.

The below "Basic Set Formulas" may seem intuitive and you may already know them—now that you "know" them, however, learn to understand, recognize, and do them on purpose.

BASIC SET FORMULAS

Toprock-Footwork-Freeze – The most fundamental of the sets. While you arguably don't need power in your set, by doing tops, footwork, and ending in a freeze, you'll put together a complete set. This formula is difficult to beat, has the necessary pieces for a full set, and will look good.

Toprock-Power-Footwork-Freeze – One of the hardest sets to beat because it has all the pieces. You'll be surprised at how well you can do at a jam by using this formula—Issei from Foundnation won R-16 multiple times just by using this single method of constructing sets, and Victor from The Squadron/MF Kidz often employs this formula.

Toprock-Footwork-Power-Freeze – This formula is similar to the above in that it has all the pieces and is hard to beat, but it tends to have a bit more texture because you'll need to figure out different ways to get into power.

Toprock-Power-Freeze – The basic "powermover" formula. This is extremely effective in crew battles, but tends to be difficult to win in formats with fewer people (i.e. 1v1s, 2v2s). Be aware that if you use this, there are many judges that may mark you down because you didn't do footwork and "that's not bboying/bgirling" (or so they would say). If this formula speaks to you, I encourage you to push the limits and make it as effective as possible.

Toprock-Freeze-Footwork-Freeze – A set with more "texture." While still relatively basic in terms of on-paper construction, this is a formula that can be hard to make flow. Play with this and learn how to incorporate different weapons in different parts of your dance.

Building Your Own Sets – Once you've mastered each of the above sets and can do them at your own discretion, it is time to develop your own rounds. The above are supposed to be a starting point so you can learn to transition between things. Add as many pieces as you like, but remember—keep it coherent! You're telling a story, so tell it well.

A Note About Doing Two "Sets" in a Round – It is not okay to do one of the above sets, get back up once you've finished, start toprocking again, and then go into another set. Many talented bboys/bgirls do this, and many continue to get away with it. While you can win battles by doing two sets, you'll put together a much more coherent and powerful story by not starting over. Be intentional about all things.

DEVELOPING MORE COMPLEX ROUNDS

Once you've mastered the above rounds, you can work on building more complex rounds and adding more ideas and concepts into your dance. I've included a number of things to think about below— note that I may have left things out and this is only a starting point for you to begin to build your dancing.

Texture – When I say texture, I refer to the different ways that you can move in a set. This encompasses level changing, slides, spins, moving both ways, jumping, vibrating, tempo changes—anything that will break up the monotony of a generic set.

Consider a landscape—while a flat landscape with nothing but dirt is beautiful in its own right, think of how much more interesting a view is with texture, be it mountains, forest, or ocean.

Whatever texture you decide to use in your set, be intentional, and build a good view.

Take Downs – Take downs are moves that you use to enter your floorwork or powermoves. This can be anything from a kick start to a knee drop to the typical "powermove stance." You must first learn all the basic take downs and learn how to do them well. Once you've developed a strong vocabulary, develop unique take downs. These should have a focus on tempo, strength, explosiveness, or finesse. If you're going into floorwork, pay attention to the music. If you're using freezes, highlight your strength and control. If doing power, do something unique. In battle settings, try to do a different take down every round so as not to become predictable.

Level Changes – Level changes are an excellent way to add diversity to your rounds. Moving up and down in power moves, doing level changes with your foot and floorworks, and doing freezes on multiple levels adds visual diversity to what you are doing. Be intentional about how you use your level changes.

Do note that it is not alright to start a round, go on the floor, and reset in a full toprock set. Not only does this hurt the continuity and coherency of your round, but you'll look lost. Resetting into toprock is not an acceptable "level change."

Jumps – Doing airborne moves is a very dynamic form of texture. Flips, powermoves in the air, and hops are one way of doing this, but consider simply doing a move you already know, and making it airborne. Look at Pickup from EXG/Kosher Flavor for a good example of this. He does jumps in everything from his toprock to floorwork and freezes, and even "jumps" in some powermoves you might not normally consider for jumps.

Traveling Moves – Slides are a good way to travel across the floor, but consider that you can do any move as a traveling move. Powermoves, footwork, even freezes can travel. Take moves that you've already developed and figure out a way to move in different directions with them. Not only does this help with the way you use the space in a cypher or battle, but it will add a literal dimension to your dance that creates dynamism.

Moves Both Ways – It is important to learn to do moves both ways. While it might not be a practical use of your time to learn how to do strong airchairs on both arms, or maintain your powermoves at equal strength, it is important to have the fundamentals on both sides. For advanced powermoves and freezes, note that it is usually beneficial to develop your strong side and push that movement as far as possible.

How far you want to push your reverse moves is up to you, but I highly encourage you to learn your footwork and at least basic power and freezes on both sides. From there, be intentional about developing movement both ways in your sets. If you're constantly rotating in one direction, you'll begin to look monotonous.

Sumo from Rock So Fresh is an excellent example of one who can make moves look amazing in any direction. He often uses direction changes to add texture to his set—while the viewer might not always be able to articulate what he is doing, his packaging creates high levels of subliminal dopeness.

Fakies – Fakies are a method to exploit the element of surprise in very small ways during your set. You set your opponent, the judges, or the crowd up with an expectation that you're going to move in one direction, when in reality you do another movement. While advanced transitions should be linking two moves in a way that is not intuitive, doing a fakie is simply setting up an expectation that you're going to do a particular move, and then breaking that expectation.

Kido from Extraordinary Gentlemen has at the same time some of the most advanced and subliminal fakies that you can find in a dancer—he'll often set as if he's going to do power and instead, do an advanced transition. Likewise, he'll float to his head as if he'll do a headspin or head freeze, but then transition into a different move. Watch his movements carefully to understand this.

Directing Your Energy (Basics) – When utilizing different texture in your rounds, pay attention to where you're directing your energy—if you're battling, you'll want to do your moves toward your opponent as a sign that you are engaging them. Note, however, that doing your moves facing your opponent the entire time can become boring—direct your energy in different ways and control it. Wherever you chose to send your energy in a round, be intentional. More about directing your energy in the Fire Book.

Physicality – Some moves, particularly in Strong Style, and in the Tricks and Blow Up style require great physicality. You can use moves that appear very strong to intimidate your opponent and show off to the crowds and judges. Keep in mind that these are inherently different than power transitions and freeze combos that require high levels of finesse. Look at bboys like Jibaku, Yosshu, and Darkness (circa 2004-2007) for examples of this.

Power Transitions – When using power moves (especially in a battle), understand that there are two key things that make your power impressive—one of which is your form. After your form, come your transitions. Rather than simply doing continuous windmills or flares, add transitions between moves to make the combo impressive. From there, develop your own unique combos and transitions. Use the ideas from other pieces of "texture" that you've developed to try new concepts. As M-Pact and Shyism have said, try to combine two powermoves in a way that doesn't seem intuitive and make it work.

Tempo Changes – Tempo changes are a great way to add texture to your set and break up your rounds. More obvious ways of doing this can be seen in bboys like Toshiki, Pocket, and Issei's powermove combos (slow to fast airflares, halos). You can, however, show this in your toprock and groundwork. Especially with your toprock and directed floorwork, changing your tempo will make you seem in control. Hitting every snare in your toprock will become monotonous—changing things up occasionally will highlight your control.

Angles in Moves – When starting to develop your own style and texture, consider adding different angles in your moves. Consider looking at a particular bboy/bgirl that you like—you could probably tell who they are if you watched a silhouette of them dancing. This is because of the unique angles that they give off when they dance.

While ballet and jazz dancers strive to have perfect lines and proper form, as a bboy/bgirl you should always look for the line that expresses yourself honestly. An excellent example of a bboy who has been intentional about developing his dance-lines is Ken Masters from The Freak Show. Pay special attention to his toprock and footwork form.

Developing Form – Form is another important piece of your dancing that you must pay attention to. While there is no technical right or wrong in bboying/bgirling, there are certainly things that look good and things that do not look good. When developing your form, be intentional. If you choose to flex or point your toes in freezes, bend or straighten your legs in power, or do flowy or choppy footwook, it doesn't matter—you should, however, be intentional about what you do and it should be an honest expression of yourself.

If you chose to develop a form that is not "standard," recognize that there are certain realities with how you will be perceived. For instance, many inexperienced bboys/bgirls tend not to flex their toes in freezes, and they tend to do flat-handed footwork. If you decide that this form speaks to you, be aware of how you'll be perceived when you do it.

Finishing Moves – This refers not to "kill moves" in the sense of moves that will absolutely destroy your opponent, but rather, moves that you can finish your set with. You must develop a series of finishing moves that you can use at the end of your round, no matter how good or poorly you feel your round has gone to that point. These should be moves that you can hit even when tired. Finishing moves should either cap off a good round, or help you end with a sense of control in a bad round. Bboys with strong finishing moves are Freakazoid from The Freak Show and Kido from EXG.

TEXTURE DRILLS

The following are a number of drills that you can use to practice the above texture concepts. These sets don't have to be perfect—the idea is to start working towards applying different types of texture in your dance and breaking out of your normal way of doing things. These drills are best performed when you're able to work with crewmembers or friends—you'll be able to build from one another's energy and ideas. Spontaneity is encouraged.

Level Changes – Include three or more in your round.

Spins – Include three or more spins in your round. Spins do not mean rotations of powermoves, but full 360 degree turns. Headspins, 90s, 2000s, knee spins, backspins, standing spins, and spins in the air are basic examples.

Slides – Include three or more in your round. Travel as much as possible.

No 6-Steps – Or make it more difficult and simply do a full round with no footwork.

No Sweeps/Hooks – Footwork is ok, but no sweeps and no hooks. Try to make your set flow without them.

No Using Your Back/Head – Easily done for a footwork round. Try to do a round of power and freezes with no back/head.

Power Starts That Aren't Power Starts – No generic power starts—you must do power from footwork, floorwork, flips, spins, freezes, or think of another way.

CCs/Sweeps/Hooks – Chose one of the three and do an entire round composed only of ccs, sweeps, or hooks.

Use Your Clothes – Practice dancing by using your clothes as props. Try to get more creative than simply brushing dust off yourself—play with it!

Use Shapes/Body Angles – Choose a shape and make the different parts of your body manifest the shape. Do a triangle set, a square set, a circle set. Try to combine and make things up.

Use Jumps – Do airborne moves three times in your round.

Traveling Moves – Use patterns that travel three times in your round.

Reverse Moves – Do an entire round going your opposite way. Also, try going back and forth between your dominant and non-dominant ways.

Figure 8's – Do a round with different figure 8 motions. Don't limit yourself to just footwork.

THE BOOK OF WATER

THE BOOK OF WATER

In the Water Book, I discuss the more intangible things surrounding bboying/bgirling. This section makes up the core of my Heiho and must be fully understood. Although the concepts are difficult and I may have left things out, with a genuine attitude and willingness to learn, the truth should become self-evident.

In the *Tao Te Ching*, a classic Chinese text on Taoism, water becomes an analogy for the Way. Much like the Way or the Tao, water can permeate everything and does so naturally. Similarly, the Way is all around us—it is in all things—and it does so without an intentional sense of "doing." You should strive to perfect the Way in all things, and become able to do so without conscious thought—simply do by doing.

The Concept of "Munen Muso" or "doing without conscious thought" is one of the most important segments in the Water Book. You must read and understand this fully.

ON BEING LIKE WATER (AND HOW BBOYS/BGIRLS MISINTERPRET IT)

As I said above, water is an analogy for the Way. Bruce Lee is often quoted as saying "Be like water," and we as bboys have adopted this mantra for our own style. I must, however, comment that in "being like water," we need to go beyond the literal. Bboys/bgirls tend to think that being like water means to flow in our dancing, to be flexible, and to adapt to our surroundings (water takes the shape of its container). This interpretation is faulty because it is too literal.

In being like water, we should accomplish these things without conscious thought. We as beings should permeate existence through our dance—thus as a dancer on the Path, you can have a sort of transcendental experience along this line of thinking. You must exercise Heiho and follow the Way diligently, as to execute things without conscious thought. In doing these things, you will be like water.

ON PRACTICING

> "Practicing a thousand days is said to be discipline, and practicing ten thousand days is said to be refining." -Musashi

Always be practicing. I'm an advocate of breaking up the way you practice so that you don't become monotonous or fall into a rut. It is important to develop flexibility, but you must keep a consistent practice schedule. Depending on what you are trying to accomplish through your practice, control your environment. Whatever your goal, keep a consistent schedule. Taking days off to heal is fine, but unless you have a major injury, you should not take weeks off. You must always be on the Path.

MORE ABOUT UNDERSTANDING THE WAY AND HEIHO

> "To beat one opponent is to beat 1000. To know one thing is to know 1000." -Musashi

Recognize that in truly understanding the Way, you will begin to understand all things. Musashi said that if you can beat one opponent, you can beat ten. If you can beat ten, you can beat 100. If you can beat 100, you can beat 1000. Similarly, to truly understand the Way, you will understand many more things.

Bboying/bgirling, like martial arts and other ways of life, is connected to all things. No matter what your Path outside of dance, you'll grow through constant practice and development. The lessons that you learn through dance are connected to all other lessons that you can learn. Continue to grow, develop, and constantly strive to see the connections in things. By understanding dance, you can create a means to understand music, art, writing, and even technical and applied sciences. You must constantly strive for growth.

I said this in the Earth Book but must reiterate—never practice just for a jam or performance. You should always be practicing— each day, each jam, win or lose, these are all steps on the Path. You should dance just as hard the week after a jam whether you won or lost, were robbed or robbed someone.

STICK-TO-IT-TIVENESS

Whether at practice or in a battle, you must be persistent. Even if you mess up, you cannot give up. Stick-to-it-iveness is one of the most important "skills" that you can have as a dancer—the person that prepares will always defeat the one who does not properly prepare. In constant practice and preparation, you will eventually succeed.

There may be times that you are deadlocked with an opponent—if your opponent is a move, yourself at practice, a rival in a cypher, or someone in a battle, you can overcome by being more persistent. You must continue to try as hard as possible.

In the same way, by developing stick-to-it-iveness in your dance, you can overcome challenges in your life. School is difficult and takes a great deal of time—by persisting, you can finish. Finding a job (and then doing the job) can require great persistence, but you can overcome. Working at relationships, finishing a creative or technical project, or doing anything worthwhile requires a great deal of effort. Do not settle for comfort. Always be growing.

ON CONTROL

I struggle to use the word "control," because I don't like the negative connotation it can take on. I don't like the thought of being "controlling" in relationships, or "controlling" other people. You must understand that when I talk about control, I mean exercising your will to decrease variables, and establish a positive environment. In getting better at doing this, you will learn to control or "manipulate" things. Never use these powers for the negative, and never use these powers to control people (unless you are in a battle).

Bboying/bgirling is a dance that highly values control. You must control yourself, the crowd, and your opponents in a battle. Although you do not pick the song, you must control your reaction to the music. Battles especially are about establishing control. If you can assert your rhythm (more on what I mean by rhythm later in the Water Book) in a battle, you will certainly be victorious. Falling into someone else's rhythm means certain defeat.

At practice, you must learn to create a best case scenario to develop moves and your style. Feel good at practice to improve your capacity to dance better and develop stronger moves—work with good people on a good floor with good music and good energy. You can also create a worst case scenario to ready yourself for negative environments at a jam—practice on a difficult floor to bad music. In this way you can develop your capacity to dance well, and you'll be ready for anything.

Your job at practice and in battles is to control the variables that exist to create a successful environment for yourself. As a student on the Path, I've won battles by controlling the environment. Learn to control yourself and others. More on this in the Fire Book.

ON ENERGY

I will discuss energy and its use in battle a great deal in the Fire Book. For our purposes now, I'll start by suggesting that energy in dancing is a real thing, although it is not necessarily tangible. Many who hear about energy in dancing will immediately dismiss it—this is foolhardy. Others will hear about energy in dancing and will equate it to "dancing hard," "moving fast," or even a similarly termed "being energetic." These are not what I mean when I discuss energy.

Yogis may call energy your "chakra," many Japanese martial artists may call it your "ki," while practitioners of Chinese martial arts may call it your "chi." I'll simply refer to it as your "energy," but it is an essential force that not only maintains you as a living thing, but drives everything that you do. From a practical level, your body is constantly metabolizing, giving off heat, and going through unconscious processes. If you've ever felt someone's presence, seen a good speaker, or been with a charismatic friend or loved one, these things all derive from that same essential energy. Learning to use your energy can help you in all aspects of your life, but for now, know that if you channel it you can use it to your advantage in dancing.

While energy does encompass "dancing hard" or moving fast, it goes beyond these things—by limiting dancing to the tangible, you'll limit your ability to use it. You can also use your energy to focus your moves on your opponent, help strike moves better, win the favor of crowds and judges, and control your dancing to a higher degree. If you lose control of your energy or don't know how to control it to begin with, you'll come off as inconsistent. If you don't know how to control your energy, you'll lose to opponents that you may be better than on a technical level. If you've ever lost a battle to someone who does "basic" things, felt yourself tire in a battle, or not gotten props for a move you normally get props for, you likely misused your energy.

You must also not "lose" to the energy of a jam or practice spot. Consider yourself as a swimmer in the ocean—your body (your energy) will generally be in an uncontrollable environment (the ocean—other people's energy). By controlling yourself, you'll be able to keep your head above water and even swim effectively through the ocean. If you panic or lose control though, you'll inevitably drown. Learn to focus your energy in everything you do.

I'll reference energy later in this chapter, and talk about it in the context of battling in the Fire Book. By knowing one thing, know 1000 things.

KEEP YOUR MIND OF THE MIDDLE WAY

By the "Middle Way," I mean balance and moderation. Unless you do so with intention, try not to be a person of extremes. If you decide you would like to walk a Path of extremes, be intentional about doing so, and pursue extreme moves as much as possible when appropriate. You should constantly be training and disciplining yourself. In pursuing the "Middle Way," though, you should strive for moderation in your lifestyle—do not practice to the point of injury. Be sure to get enough rest and food, but not too much. Don't drink until you're sick. Have your wits about you when battling and practicing. When you decide to be "extreme," or simply "go with it," by giving yourself up to your feeling, know when you are doing so and embrace those moments.

TATEMAE 建前 (PRESENTATION) VS HONNE 本音 (INTENTIONS)

Alien Ness references this concept in his book *The Art of Battle*, although he uses a different vocabulary. He discusses the fact that he has a "gangster" persona and likes to piss people off, in contrast to Poe One, who has a "gentleman" persona. These are "Tatemae" they've developed to portray an image to others.

You probably know that Tatemae and Honne exist already—you've probably kept something secret or put on a different face for friends, family, teachers, or a significant other. The important thing here is intention—you as a bboy/bgirl should be intentional about what you show to others and what you have inside. Use this to your advantage. When it benefits you, show confidence. When it benefits you, be nice to your opponents. This may sound manipulative, but it is a technique that you must learn—a part of "battling outside of the battle." You're already competing with your opponents before you enter the jam and even after the last person has finished their rounds. You must construct your Tatemae with intention in the bboy/bgirl scene to be victorious.

Please also understand that I'm not advocating for using Tatemae as a means of manipulation—you should be honest and transparent with your relationships and your loved ones. I am, however, advocating for higher levels of self-awareness, and an understanding of how you present yourself to others. You must understand this fully.

KAN 勘 (SEEING INTO OR THROUGH) VS KEN 見 (SEEING THE SUPERFICIAL)

While Tatemae and Honne have to do with how others perceive you, Kan and Ken have to do with how you perceive others. Know that you should never take anything at face value. You should learn to think for yourself—never consider anything you see or hear as "right" or "wrong" at first glance. Rather, start from a place of neutrality and decide for yourself whether things are right or wrong.

Even without knowing it, people will be putting forth a Tatemae and holding in a Honne—by reading these things with intention, you will have an advantage. Look for inconsistencies in other people's Tatemae. Pick up on non-verbal communication, pay attention, and think of the big picture. When you put things together in perspective, you will begin to see with feeling (Kan), rather than simply seeing with your eyes (Ken).

ON FLEXIBILITY

When bboys/bgirls think to "be like water," they often consider flexibility a central tenant of the analogy. Although limiting the analogy to this way of thinking can be destructive and does not take the idea to its full meaning, matters of flexibility are certainly important and worth discussion. While physical flexibility will make you a stronger dancer and help prevent injury, by being emotionally and spiritually flexible as a dancer, you will create a stronger self.

Both practices and jams have a huge variety of environments. You may be dancing on any number of floors, to any type of music, with crowds of varying size, in different venues, in different time-zones, at different times of day, and with different energy levels (and of course, there are still many more variables). Learning to perform effectively in any of these environments is a key to being like water.

Rest assured, this is not something you can immediately "do," but you must work to develop. As I mention above, there are different variables that you can manipulate in your day to day practice. Dance on different floors to different types of music with different people. Wear different clothes and learn what moves are best suited to what environment. Much like physical flexibility is developed, you can develop the flexibility to dance effectively in any environment. When you're "not feeling it," this is a matter of your inflexibility. You must understand this fully.

"A POSITION IS NOT A POSITION" OR "A MOVE IS NOT A MOVE"

In bboying/bgirling, we often emphasize hitting a move, getting to a specific freeze, or doing a specific spin. As a result, we also often get sloppy about the things that we do before or after the move.

By asserting that a position is not a position or a move is not a move, I mean to say that we shouldn't place the entire focus of our round on just a move, but should be intentional both about the way that we package it, and how we transition in and out of it. Typically, when we focus so heavily on just doing a move, the entirety of our round will suffer as a result.

Eddie Styles talks about this same concept when discussing musicality—rather than "hitting" beats and being done with it, we as dancers should "ride" beats. You can do nearly the same moves, but simply maintain your flow. Do not end with just "hitting" your moves, but "ride" out of them the same way as you would with the music. You must understand this fully.

MUNEN MUSO (無念無想) OR "WITHOUT CONSCIOUS THOUGHT"

Munen Muso is one of the most important concepts not just in the Water Book, but in my school of Heiho more generally. In Western thought, we'd think of "Munen Muso" as "being in the zone," or getting wrapped up in a moment and executing flawlessly without conscious thought.

Munen Muso is the epitome of the Way in that we simply exist, we simply do—and we manifest Art and the Way without thought. If you've ever "been in the zone," or "been into it," you've probably experienced something similar to Munen Muso.

Munen Muso is fundamentally different than "blanking out" in your round. True, you're operating without thinking in both cases, but in the "blanking out" stage, you've engaged your body's "fight or flight" response, and this is a result of panic. You have no control.

When you experience Munen Muso, you'll have a heightened sense of awareness. You'll understand how your body moves, when you can execute what, and where the music is (i.e. you might hit beats perfectly you didn't experientially know were coming). Psychologists have studied this phenomenon—some declare that this is actually an extremely intense form of focus .

You can increase your capacity to fall into the Munen Muso mindset—the best way to do this is adhering to the Heiho that I've outlined. You must constantly be practicing mindfully so that your body will be ready to execute when the situation comes. You must also understand the Way so that you can fall into the mental state without panic. The more you work, the stronger this will become. When you execute with Munen Muso, your opponent will be irrelevant—you'll be able to beat anyone.

UTSU (打つ) VS ATARU (当たる)

This is a difficult concept but one that will greatly help you on your Path. Consider it an application of Munen Muso.

While "utsu" and "ataru" basically have the same denotation (to hit), they have different connotations. "Utsu" means to "deal a blow with conscious thought." To "Ataru" has the meaning of "to come by," and generally means to "strike without thinking," or simply to "just do it." "Ataru" is a physical manifestation of Munen Muso.

In terms of bboying/bgirling, consider "Utsu" as just doing a move, but without intention—you can throw a move but maybe not hit it well, it isn't necessarily directed, and there is no feeling. In the fact of focusing so much on the move itself you actually take away from it.

If you're dancing and you're in the zone (Munen Muso), you generally have a natural sense of what you can and can't do, and this is when you have the capacity to execute strong moves without thinking about them so much. The mental emphasis is not on the move itself, but just being or just dancing.

Put simply, you must learn to "ataru," or do moves by passing through them. Learn to get in the zone. Rather than just hitting your moves, learn how to "be" and manifest your moves through that fact. You will gain a greater understanding of this through constant practice.

ON UNDERSTANDING
YOUR OPPONENTS

> "It is said that if you know your enemies and know yourself, you will not be imperiled in a hundred battles; if you do not know your enemies but do know yourself, you will win one and lose one; if you do not know your enemies nor yourself, you will be imperiled in every single battle." -Sun Tzu

Sun Tzu's quotation from *The Art of War* is relatively straightforward—if you know your enemy and yourself, you've got nothing to worry about. If you don't have that awareness, you'll be at great risk.

This is as much a note about developing self-awareness— knowing your own weaknesses and shortcomings, playing to your strengths—as it is about preparation and manipulation. You must seek to manipulate the variables of a battle or your general environment to control your enemy to your advantage. You can do this by understanding your enemy.

Get to know your enemy. Understand what they like and don't like. Learn about what songs they like. Watch their videos online— understand when they kill it, and learn their bad habits. When you know these things, you can control them. Not only can you be prepared in a battle and call out their moves (if you decide to), you can learn to manipulate variables. You can do moves before them, or prepare strong counters. If you know they like a part of the song you're battling to, you can go out and steal that part of the song. Set yourself up for success by manipulating the variables.

A NOTE ON PRE-REGISTRATION AND KNOWING YOUR ENEMY

I fundamentally disagree with pre-registering for a jam online unless you absolutely have to. If your opponents pre-register, this gives you the chance to research and understand them better—you'll be better prepared.

In pre-registering for a jam, you give your enemies the ability to research your recent battles, understand your habits, and more importantly, mentally prepare themselves to stand across from you in a battle. If you don't pre-register and let your opponents know that you're coming to a jam, you'll be able to take them by surprise and throw them off. This will give you an upper hand—you should always take advantage of the element of surprise.

A NOTE ON PRACTICE VIDEOS AND KNOWING YOUR ENEMY

Recently, many bboys/bgirls accrue fame through posting videos online of themselves practicing. While this will help you generate popularity through the community of e-boys/e-girls (electronic bboys/bgirls), this will not help you win battles, or generate long term respect. E-boys/e-girls tend to focus on the short term, while true bboys/bgirls will be there for the bigger picture.

By posting practice videos online showing yourself in a "best case scenario" environment, you will reveal to your enemies what you are capable of—unfortunately, while this may help you with the "intimidation factor," when you inevitably don't hit the same moves in the less-than-perfect-environment of a battle, your opponents and the judges will consider you as not meeting your potential.

Again, the element of surprise is a real factor when you battle. Practice your moves in secret, and pull them out when your enemies and judges are not expecting them. They will have a bigger impact and intimidate more than if you had shown them earlier.

It is occasionally acceptable to post practice videos if you wish to share something with the community with no intention but to share. Be careful with how much footage you show and how often you show it. If you're working on a move that is simply too difficult to do in a battle and you never intend to use it, it may be appropriate to "intimidate" with that move through videos.

Please also note that I believe trailers, battle footage, and art or concept videos are meant to be shared, and the internet and social media are excellent tools for building our reputations as dancers. I'm advocating against posting practice videos that will detract from your success in the long run.

APPLYING WATER CONCEPTS TO YOUR DANCE

ON THE "FLOWING WATER BLOW"

The "Flowing Water Blow" is an attack that you can utilize when your opponent attacks at a single tempo. The point here is to demonstrate that you have a higher level of control than the person you're battling. If your opponent appears too energetic and out of control, come out slowly and toprock slowly on beat to demonstrate that you can move at multiple speeds. When the music changes appropriately, or you move to the floor, speed up your tempo to show your level of control. Doing this will not only draw attention to your ability to control yourself, but it will make your opponent look as if they were nervous and too hectic.

The point of this move is to simulate a river or ocean in its different states of flowing. Consider a river that moves quickly in the rapids, but slows down to a crawl and is very calm in certain parts. Your dancing can model this flow.

COMPARING THE HEIGHT OF BAMBOO

You will often see bboys/bgirls doing this in battles—it often manifests itself as a stare-down or a mean mug. "Comparing the height of bamboo" is to intimidate the opponent by showing yourself as larger, stronger, or meaner (and not always physically larger or stronger, mind you). In bboying/bgirling in particular, size doesn't always matter for the intimidation factor—you can choose to "compare the height of bamboo" simply with your eyes or your demeanor.

Comparing the height of bamboo is a good way not just to mentally attack your opponent, but to show the crowd and judges that you are confident.

Be aware that some people will make a joke of comparing the height of bamboo, or will not respond. Be intentional about how you use this, and develop your own style for doing so. Beyond all things, know that displaying confidence in battle is key, but because of the crowd and judges in a bboy/bgirl battle, you don't always have to work directly against your opponent for this to be successful.

THE ORDER OF OPPONENTS WHEN FIGHTING ALONE

There are different situations when you'll be battling alone—you should be able to control and manipulate your opponents to work to your advantage in these situations. Consider historical battles when few stood against many—The Battle of Thermopylae, Musashi's fight against the House of Yoshioka, Jonathan against the Philistines—there are any number of such battles in history, and they all emphasize the fact that with the right tactics, few can triumph against many.

In order to make this effective, you must control as many variables as possible. You may not be able to control the floor or music, but by knowing your enemies, you can certainly play to your own strengths. Generally, crowds, MCs, and DJs will root for you if you're battling the many by yourself—the only real people in the peripheral you may have to overcome are the judges if you're entering a judged battle.

One Versus Two – Manipulate who goes out and how you respond to them. The most important thing here is to know your enemy. If you are in a four round battle, keep your energy high. Emphasize what you can do that they can't, and do your best to point out their flaws. Do not under any circumstances sit, squat, or put your hands on your knees. You must demonstrate not only technical but physical superiority to make it clear how much better you are—even if you aren't. The trick isn't to be the better dancer, but to convince everyone in your surrounding (including your enemies) that you are the better dancer.

Changing tempo works well in a one versus two situation to demonstrate control, but generally speaking, never end on a slow note. You should end strong and with energy—if you show even the least bit of slowing down in this situation, people will interpret it as you being tired. If it means pacing yourself and going slower to begin with, you must find ways to finish with high energy.

One (or Two) Versus a Crew – Generally speaking, if you are in a situation battling a crew by yourself, no one will take you seriously—they'll assume that you won't have the stamina to hold the entire battle and typically they'll hold back. Use this against them. If you really intend on winning the battle, keep your energy high through your latter rounds. Before your opponent knows it, you will have silently won two or three rounds and they will not be able to come back against you. Under no circumstances can you appear tired. Battling a crew is more a psychological game—they won't consider you a threat until it is too late—you must know and take advantage of this.

Controlling the Judges – The judges are the hardest obstacle to overcome when entering a judged battle by yourself. Many judges simply won't let you pass prelims because you are battling by yourself—this is faulty, as you should be judged (as closely to) objectively based upon the merit of your rounds, but you must also realize that this is a reality of battling alone.

Your goal in battling alone is to convince the judges that they must put you through no matter what. What this means is that you must throw some of your best material at the onset of the jam. If entering a 2v2 alone, both your rounds must be seamless and demonstrate that you can utilize a variety of weapons. If entering a 3v3 alone, all rounds must be seamless and you cannot tire.

If you are able to pass prelims, judges will tend to start judging round by round, so it will become easier to defeat your opponents. The difficulty is forcing them to pay attention to you from the outset, and you must do so by not holding back from the very beginning.

DANCING TO THE MUSIC

As I've mentioned before, the music is one of (if not the) most important aspects of dancing. The music that you practice to, battle to, and even listen to in your off time will influence the way you dance. You must be aware of what the music does to you and be intentional about exploring music that allows you to express yourself honestly.

You must also learn to interpret music. Bboy Kazu from I Love Footwork said that he attempts to "sing the song with [his] body" when he dances. To do this on a practical level, you must learn what movements make sense with what sounds. While Indian Steps may make sense for a typical snare, a drum roll could be rapid foot movement, a baseline could create upper body movement, a horn could be a slide or a spin, or a guitar riff could be rapid hand movements.

You must experiment to find out what moves make sense with the sounds of a song—watch both Kazu (I Love Footwork) and Y-Not from Rock Steady Crew to get a sense of what this looks like.

Once you've begun to understand in practice what this looks and feels like, you must work to make it natural. Let your body play the song naturally, and interpret different aspects of the music fluidly. Remember that "A Move is Not a Move," and you should take each move as a transition to the next—you're not stopping your flow but maintaining the rhythm of the song. You must understand this fully.

ON DEVELOPING UNIQUE MOVES

While I discuss labbing and practicing in the Earth Book, I want to add a bit of conceptual (Water) framework to the thought of creating moves. While it is inevitable that you will copy the basic moves that you see as a beginner (i.e. learn Indian Steps, basic footwork or floorwork, foundational power), you must learn to add a unique twist to these. Strive to do something that has never been done before, and recognize that you don't always have to look to "bboying" or "bgirling" for inspiration. If you have any other hobbies or any other interests, develop moves from those sets of inspirations.

How might a famous painter dance? What would a jazz musician do if they started dancing spontaneously in the middle of a music piece? What would a sculptor dance like when crafting a piece? What does a calligraphy stroke look like and how could you translate it to dance? I believe that you must cultivate a wide love of the arts to succeed as a dancer and a person, but your inspiration doesn't have to stop there.

Consider skaters, football players, martial artists, construction workers, computer programmers, accountants...do any of these professions have something you can draw upon? The possibilities are limitless, and you only stop yourself and your growth by thinking that you can't draw inspiration from other areas of life.

ON GOING BLANK IN BATTLES

Under extreme situations of stress, bboys/bgirls sometimes go blank in battles. This can be caused by nervousness, a high level opponent using their energy to disrupt your concentration, or by getting flustered from a mistake. Even if you're not the type of bboy/bgirl who typically goes blank in a battle, it is still good to have a backup.

The key to salvaging sets when you go blank in a battle is to have a "go-to" move that you can execute under any circumstance. This is a double edged sword though, because to have such a move can become a crutch. Your go-to moves, however, can also save you in bad situations—develop these moves knowing that they can be a weakness as well.

As with the set construction theory of breaking your moves into pieces (beginning, middles, ends), you should have one or two end moves that are strong and that you can use at any time. Practice these diligently to the point where they become muscle memory and you can use them at any time or at any point during your set. If you blank out in a battle, you'll be able to allow your body to default to these moves from practicing them so much, or you can train your thoughts on this one move in situations of distress.

ON RHYTHM IN BBOYING/BGIRLING

There are obvious rhythms in bboying/bgirling—the rhythms of the music, the rhythm of your body or your moves as you dance, or the rhythms of the jam itself. It is important to understand that there are more subtle rhythms to what is happening around you as you battle and bboy/bgirl. It is almost detrimental to discuss the "rhythm" in bboying/bgirling, because we immediately think of music and the rhythm of our bodies articulating the music. What I mean here, though, is the underlying rhythm of everything that we do, and how it relates to cosmic "music."

Consider this—have you ever been in a battle and realized that you were winning or losing? There was likely a momentum to the situation that you felt at the time you couldn't control. Likewise, have you felt a good or bad practice and let the momentum carry you either way? Have you ever simply "gone with it" in another situation outside of dance? That feeling that you have is the inherent rhythm of each of these situations.

There is a definite rhythm that you exert when winning a battle, and likewise, there is a rhythm to losing a battle. There is a rhythm to a good and bad practice, and there is a rhythm to confidence and nervousness. On the physical level, this has to do with your bodily processes (sometimes signs of nervousness), along with your breathing, and your output of energy. The rhythm that different situations create is an amalgam of you, the space, the music, and those around you as "instruments" creating these rhythms.

To become successful in bboying/bgirling and in battles, you must learn to recognize these rhythms, what they feel like, and how to articulate the good ones (winning, practicing well, vibing out, enjoying yourself). If you develop a good rhythm at a jam or practice, remember what it "sounds" like and do your best to recreate it as much as possible. Likewise, when you "hear" the rhythm of losing, practicing poorly, or not having fun, you must "change the song" and develop methods to change the rhythm. In a battle you can typically override a negative rhythm by changing strategy. At practice, you can change the music and method of your approach. You must learn how to do this for yourself through constant practice and experimentation.

When I feel myself or my crew falling into a negative rhythm at practice, I'll purposely do something to disrupt that negative rhythm—I'll make us battle, go rounds, run drills, or change the music. Likewise, if you feel a negative rhythm developing in a battle, change your tactics. Understand rhythm through practice and study.

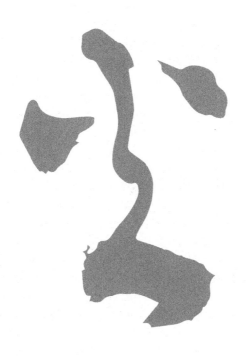

THE BOOK OF FIRE

THE BOOK OF FIRE

The Fire Book is a discussion of battles. My goal here is to give you the tools to be successful in judged battles. I'll also discuss cypher battles, though not in as much detail. While the emphasis here is on judged battle, I do think cypher battles are extremely important and deserve discussion, although they are a much different creature than judged battles. I also discuss jams in this section, as judged battles usually occur in the context of a jam.

The idea of the Fire Book is to give you the tools to understand battles and know how to conduct yourself with fidelity. The Fire Book also uses two primary frameworks related to battle: one specifically about bboying/bgirling, and one about the ideas regarding battles in general (not necessarily related to dance). Think of these frameworks as the "what'" and the "why" of the Fire Book. Understanding the ideas about bboying/bgirling (the "what") without understanding the larger conceptual ideas (the "why") will give you tools to operate well in certain environments, but it will not teach you to think on your own. You must understand both.

THE IMPORTANCE OF HAVING A RIVAL

Whether you have one or many, it is important to have rivals. Of course, keep your rivalry on friendly terms as much as you can (Hip Hop is supposed to be based in positivity, after all), but you and your rival should constantly be pushing each other to new heights. Many things in the universe operate in binaries or in revolving systems—this is the natural way of things. More often than not, if you stick to the Way and do your best to be competitive, you'll eventually run into a rival. Cultivate the relationship—battle with and against the person, practice with them and then practice more than them in secret (because they'll be doing the same!). Do your best to cultivate your rivalry with someone who really loves the dance and you'll be able to improve much more than if you walked the Path alone. You don't have to walk the same Path exactly, but your Way will intersect at points—this will make the journey all the more worthwhile.

ON COMBAT (BATTLES)

Many would argue that Hip Hop has progressed so quickly and continues to grow because of the competitive aspect ascribed to it. In every element, practitioners do their best to improve to assert their superiority. You must understand that battling is a cornerstone of the art form.

If you'd like to be a Platonic practitioner of the dance (in other words, dance for the love and not to compete), that's fine, but know that battling is an inherent part of the system of bboying/bgirling. You should also recognize that even if you aren't battling against someone across the cypher from you, every time you dance you are battling against yourself. Use this to grow.

ON CONTROL IN BATTLES: MANIPULATING VARIABLES

I've talked about control in the Water Book, and I'll discuss control more throughout the Fire Book. I must, however, explicitly state that control in battle is highly valuable. If you can demonstrate control in a battle, you will never have to worry about the outcome—even if you lose a battle, you'll gain respect and people will recognize you. The reality is that you may also win battles simply by demonstrating control over yourself and your opponent.

You can draw attention to your level of control through many methods—by demonstrating a tempo change, by doing a move better than your opponent, or simply by pointing out a deficiency that your opponent may have in their dance. However you choose to do so, control is a hugely important part of battle and you must learn to manipulate the variables around you to maximize your chance to win.

Consider a basic algebraic formula. With one variable, it is easy to solve. With two variables, it becomes more difficult. When you have to solve a problem for more variables, the problem becomes more difficult and more varied. Think of battles in the same way—the more variables you can control, the simpler the "problem" will be.

Control Yourself – As many people discuss, and I've mentioned before, battles are ultimately a test of yourself, and a battle against yourself—if you can control yourself, you need not fear the outcome.

The two major facets that you must control are your mental state and your physical state. Control your mental state through constant practice and discipline. Fully understand the Water Book and my Heiho and conduct yourself calmly in tumultuous situations. Do not ever lose control or put yourself in a compromising situation. Be ready for the worst and practice how to respond. Stay calm.

The other major facet to control is your physical state. Often in times of extreme stress, your body may want to rebel—you may blank mentally or you may be tired, dehydrated, or hurt. You can overcome the control of your physical state through constant practice and preparation. Eat right, don't drink before a jam, and always practice. Understand how to keep your energy up through the entirety of a jam (explained below), and maintain good health. Controlling your physicality is largely a matter of preparation.

Control Your Crew – In battle, you must always have a Floor General. The Floor General is the one who decides the order of those going out in a battle, determines the strategy, and calls routines if appropriate. To properly control your crew, you must understand the moves that everyone has at their disposal, and their typical patterns of battle.

Do you have an inconsistent bboy/bgirl on your squad? Is someone a big risk taker that could self-destruct or have huge payoff? Is there a consistent bboy/bgirl that will always win their round? Who matches up well with the bboys/bgirls on the opposing squad? Consider all these things when determining who to send out.

Beyond the literal fact of controlling how your crew goes out and who is battling who, you must also control your crew's energy. As the leader, your crew will look to you for morale. They'll expect you to keep cool and make good decisions, even in the heat of battle. You must approach every battle like you can win and give it your all—never approach a battle thinking you're going to lose. Even if you believe that inside, you have to display confidence. Your crew will pick up on your non-verbal communication and reflect that in their dancing. You must control them with your energy and they will give you back energy. You must understand this fully.

I talk more in-depth about the strategy of battles themselves in other parts of the Fire Book. For now, understand that you have influence over your crew and thus, influence over the outcome of the battle.

Control Your Opponent – Your opponent tends to be the most volatile variable in battle, since they will be trying to beat you. Even with the thought that they will be using their energy to defeat you, you can use their energy against them. Consider a skilled Judo practitioner—it is a well-accepted paradigm in Judo that the strongest martial artist doesn't necessarily win, but rather the one who can use their opponent's strength against them.

There are different ways to control your opponent. You can get a rise out of them by talking trash or burning them (although this may give rise to other variables), you can trick them into going out first or intimidate them by going out first yourself, or in a crew battle, you can call out one of the opponents. Additionally, you can force them to do moves (or not to do moves) based upon the round that you throw against them. You can also get into their head through intimidation or conversely by putting them too much at ease before the battle.

Whatever method you use, be intentional about how you approach your opponent, and be sure that you are the one in control—keep in mind all the time that like Fire itself, your opponent is a volatile force.

On Demonstrating Control over Your Opponent –
Demonstrating control over your opponent is easier than actually controlling your opponent. The difference is this—by "controlling your opponent," you force their hand, or create an action for them through your actions. By "demonstrating control over your opponent," you are showing to the audience and the judges that you are in control regardless of what your opponent does.

You can demonstrate control over your opponent by making it obvious that you have certain skills they do not have. If your opponent is not able to dance on beat, make it clear that you are good at dancing on beat. If your opponent struggled with a powermove or freeze that you are good at, make it clear that you are better.

Consider that this can go beyond simply the moves that you're working with. If your opponent is not good at focusing their energy, show that you are. If they are too frantic or too slow in their set, demonstrate that you have control over your speed and that they don't. By demonstrating your control you'll be able to commandeer the flow of a battle easily, and you will be able to beat bboys/bgirls who may be technically better.

Please understand that I'm not advocating for doing moves on the sidelines while your opponent is in their round (i.e. your opponent does a flip and you flip immediately after, even though it's not your turn). This will make you look uncontrolled, it is rude, and you'll waste your energy. I'm advocating for using the skills, technique, and tools that you have at your disposal in context to demonstrate your superior control. You must understand this fully.

Control the Crowd – The crowd is another variable that you must contend with in battles. If you walk into a battle and try to use your energy against the crowd, you'll surely drown—your energy will not be enough to work against the entire crowd's. Instead, you must ride their energy like a wave and use it against your opponent. Know that no matter what situation you are in (even battling a hometown hero outside of your city), the crowd will want you to kill it, because they want to see a dope battle. Give the crowd positive vibes and work with the energy that they give you, and it will reflect in the way you dance, the way the judges view you, and the way your opponent battles you.

Control the Music – Strictly speaking, the DJ controls the music. Unless the DJ knows what you like to hear and is willing to give it to you, you are at the mercy of what the DJ likes to play. You can, however, control what part of a song you dance to and ultimately what part of a song you give to your opponent. This will come by knowing the songs that each DJ plays, and if they loop them or not—with this in mind, you can take the good part of a song for yourself, and leave your opponent stuck with a bad part of the song.

The most obvious example of this is Kleju dancing to "Killing" by The Apples. While Pirat (his opponent) is technically a very good bboy, because of the nature of the song and the way Kleju danced to it, he simply does not have potential in his round to overcome the fact of the music being against him.

Control the Judges – I reject the idea that you should dance differently based upon who your judges are. You may have heard bboys/bgirls say "Oh, person X is judging, so I better do more footwork today," or "Person Y is judging so he's going to vote for the bboys with power." Any competent judge will be able to see through such facades—you should be dancing true to yourself at all times and this will reflect in the outcome of your rounds.

With that said, you can control the judges to a certain degree. Don't show them all your moves prior to the battle—use the element of surprise. Display confidence at all times. Don't be afraid to interact with the judges outside of the tournament. More than anything else, you must obliterate your opponent—you must make it so clear to the judges that you are the superior dancer that they have no choice but to vote for you. If you worry about them not paying attention, be shocking. Make it clear that you've won.

ON ENERGY IN BATTLES

Energy in battles is one of the most important facets of the competition. When you are facing opponents who are technically better, you can often commandeer the flow of a battle and win because of your energy. Do not, however, be out of control or obnoxious—make it clear that you have (and dance with) energy, and give your crew and the crowd energy. More than anything, be in control of your energy and where you are sending it. If you are low on energy or tired, be conscious of what you are doing with the energy you have and try to get energy from your crew or the crowd.

Your Energy – You can be fully in control of this. You can increase your energy reserves through training—eat right, sleep well, and take care of your body. You'll be surprised how much energy you have simply by doing this.

During a jam, you may find that your energy is different than during your day to day routine. You may be nervous, you may feel worn down, or you may feel that the different environment is hurting your energy. Prepare for this by controlling variables in practice and you'll be ready for any situation—and if you still struggle with your energy, you can at least have the mental wherewithal to deal with it properly.

When in the battle, be aware of what you do with your energy. Direct it at the opponent during your set to demonstrate focus and control. Give energy to your crewmates by giving them props and words of encouragement. Show how much energy you have by dancing well in your sets. Above all, control your energy.

Occasionally, you may want to give energy to your opponents. Alien Ness talks about this in *The Art of Battle*—while typically you want to use your energy against your opponent, if you are facing an opponent who is far below your level, you can give them good energy to win over the crowd and the judges. Whatever you do, do so with intention.

Your Opponent's Energy – Be aware of where your opponent is sending their energy. A skilled opponent will use all of their energy to defeat you—they'll be using the same concepts I talk about here. They will try to undo what you're doing and win the favor of the crowd and the judges. Don't let their energy affect you, and keep controlled and focused in your energy disbursement.

You will, however, come up against opponents with high levels of energy that don't have much control of it. Usually, these are bboys/

bgirls that focus more on executing moves and technicality than battle strategy. While these bboys/bgirls should be taken seriously because of the level of their moves and skill, you can use their energy against them. Make it clear that they have no control over their energy and demonstrate that you have focus. More often than not, by demonstrating this control you'll be able to overcome your opponent.

Your Crew's Energy – Your crew's energy can win or lose you battles. If your crew can maintain high energy and control it, you'll be able to control the flow of the battle. More than anything you must work with your crew to control the flow of your energy—do not let energy get too low when you are tired, and go with the flow when your energy is good.

As with anything, be intentional. Consider a hype crew battle, and a situation where an opposing crew kills it. Usually in a situation like that, the crowd will be hype and your natural reaction will be to throw something crazy back. If you're certain you can win, do it. If you don't have the firepower to respond with blowups though, demonstrate control—purposely slow the battle down with a controlled toprock set and then set your own pace on the floor. By controlling your crew's energy—be it high or purposely low—you can control and win battles.

COMMANDING BATTLES

I discuss many of the intangible aspects of commanding battles above. This section is a practical breakdown of how to command battles. You must know how to use your crewmembers and yourself effectively to determine the order of the battle and who you're battling against. Often when in a 2v2 or even a 3v3, it will be immediately obvious who should take which opposing dancer's round. Often though, you'll want to avoid that "natural" feeling of who should match up to who, and control the battle.

Much like a sports team has different positions, each person should have a certain role based upon what they are good at in a battle. Of course, your crew may have multiple people filling these roles, you may be missing some listed here from your crew, or you might have some of your own. Know that these are some of the basic roles filled in battles, and that others exist. We're doing this for the sake of understanding and you should ultimately create your own system that works for you and your crew.

The Floor General – The Floor General is the bboy/bgirl that makes the decisions in battle. The Floor General has the difficult role of evaluating the battle objectively while simultaneously being in the battle. They must know whether they are winning or losing, who to send out, what routines to call, and on top of that, they must dance themselves and maintain their composure after their own set. This must be a mentally strong bboy/bgirl but doesn't necessarily have to be the best dancer.

The Pacesetter – The Pacesetter is the bboy/bgirl that should go out first, or in an extended battle, go out to control the pace of the battle. Generally, these are bboys/bgirls with good style and good musicality. They'll be comfortable dancing on the floor, like dancing in front of people, and aren't easily flustered. Use them to get your crew vibe warmed up so that your more explosive dancers will feel comfortable and in control later.

The Consistent Bboy/Bgirl – The Consistent Bboy/Bgirl is the dancer who might not have crazy blow ups or crazy style, but they never do poorly—they tend to be "solid" and do sets that are "pretty good," most of the time. While most bboys/bgirls probably aren't trying to be The Consistent Bboy/Bgirl (most people want to get lots of props!) they are a huge asset to have in a battle. When your opponent throws a mediocre round or messes up, use The Consistent Bboy/Bgirl to win those rounds. Your opponent will have lost before they know what happened.

The Clutch - The Clutch is like The Consistent Bboy/Bgirl, but with power or tricks. They'll be able to blow it up and don't get easily flustered. Be aware that if you put too much pressure on The Clutch throughout the course of the jam, they may begin to wear out. Use them to win rounds when you absolutely need them, and place them towards the end of battles so you can end on a strong note.

Be aware of their energy level when guiding them in battle, and reel them back to be like The Consistent Bboy/Bgirl if they are wearing out. Better to have them do a solid set than go beyond their limits and underperform.

The Bomb – The Bomb is the bboy/bgirl on your squad who has the ability to blow shit up but often crashes or messes up. Unless you absolutely have to, try not to use The Bomb at the end of the battle—if they do mess up, it will make your crew look like a mess. Instead, throw The Bomb out in the middle of a battle (after you've controlled the pace) and let them go crazy. If they do self-destruct (as bombs sometimes do), you'll still have rounds to recover with one of your Consistent Bboys/Bgirls or The Clutch.

The Roundwinner – The Roundwinner is similar to The Clutch in that they have the capacity to do high level moves, but generally speaking, they have a stronger understanding of battle tactics and aren't easily flustered. This bboy/bgirl will be able to gauge what the opponent does and throw the appropriate amount in response—they won't burn moves on battling weak bboys/bgirls, and they'll know how to respond to strong opponents. Use the Roundwinner to control the middle of the battle or to win tie-breakers.

UNDERSTANDING YOUR CREW

The most important aspect of being the Floor General is understanding your crew and understanding who to send out at what point. I'm going to give a basic version of "Understanding Your Crew." Use your own understanding and intuition, and the meaning should come through. The idea here is to give you an example of how to evaluate your crew's assets. You should tweak this method and develop a style that works to your understanding and the strengths of your crew.

I'm going to break this down based loosely upon the "weapons" described in the Earth Book. Evaluate your crewmembers based upon the following weapons:

Toprock or General Style
Quality of Floorwork
Powermoves
Blowups

We're also going to add two other sections based on the intangible quality of their dancing:

Battle Mentality
Consistency

Then, let's evaluate the crewmembers based on a scale of one to ten. Really, whatever score you give them is arbitrary (and of course, it's subjective), but we're doing it to give you an idea of who should fill what role in the battle.

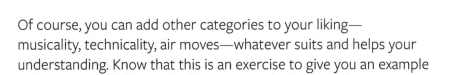

Of course, you can add other categories to your liking—musicality, technicality, air moves—whatever suits and helps your understanding. Know that this is an exercise to give you an example of crew evaluation and breaks things down to a simple level.

Also know that the examples I give below are just that: examples. They are only intended to give you an idea of how to evaluate your crew and plan for battle.

EXAMPLE 1 (2V2):

Bboy	Style	Floorwork	Power	Blowups	B.M.	Consistency
Y-Roc	7	5	7	7	7	7
Finny Fin	8	8	4	5	7	8

From the example above, you can see that I rate myself as a well-balanced and consistent bboy, but I might be somewhat lacking in the floorwork department. Fin, on the other hand, is a stylish bboy but might lack power and blowups. We both have solid battle mentality and consistency.

In this case, Fin would fit the role of Pacesetter, while I'd be The Consistent Bboy (or possibly The Clutch, in a 2v2 situation). As a result, we'd want Fin to go out first in 2v2s to build the case for our crew, while I'd take the second position. Unless we match up particularly well against our opponents or I really like the song, this will almost always be the case.

EXAMPLE 2 (3V3):

Bboy	Style	Floorwork	Power	Blowups	B.M.	Consistency
Y-Roc	7	5	7	7	7	7
Finny Fin	8	8	4	5	7	8
Neat-O	6	5	9	9	6	5

In example two, Fin and I would probably be playing similar roles as we did in a 2v2. Because of his good style, Fin would be the Pacesetter, and I would be The Consistent Bboy. Because Neat-O is still relatively consistent and has solid battle mentality, he probably wouldn't qualify as The Bomb, but rather The Clutch. In a 3v3, Neat-O and I could split the 2nd and 3rd position, depending on the song and who we match well against. If one of us is getting tired, we'd probably put the more energetic person at the end of the battle to leave off on a good note. Again, because his style and floorwork is so much better than Neat-O's or mine, Fin would almost always be the Pacesetter.

In that rare case that Neat-O or I needed or wanted to go first (the song demanded it, the judges or host called for a four or five round battle), we'd need to put Fin in the middle.

EXAMPLE 3 (4V4):

Bboy	Role	Style	Floor-work	Power	Blowups	B.M.	Consistency
Y-Roc	Consist	7	5	7	7	7	7
Finny Fin	Paceset	8	8	4	5	7	8
Neat-O	Clutch	6	5	9	9	6	5
Zick	Round Winner	8	8	7	8	7	7

In the case of a 4v4 with the four of us in a squad, I've assigned the roles above. Since he is extremely versatile and can play any role, we can assign Zick the role of "Roundwinner." Generally our strategy doesn't change too much—Finny Fin will set the pace, I'll fill the 2nd or 3rd slot, Neat-O would split the 3rd or 4th spot, and Zick would fill spots 2-4, depending on the situation.

We'd use Zick more towards the middle of the battle if we felt it was close and my consistency wasn't enough to make it clear that we were winning. If we were winning but not blowing the opponent out, we could use Zick in the 4th slot to seal the deal. We'd still want Neat-O to go 3rd or 4th to end on a strong note, and my consistency at 2nd or 3rd would usually be able to maintain the flow of the battle in our direction.

EXAMPLE 4 (CREW V. CREW)

Bboy	Role	Style	Floor-work	Power	Blowups	B.M.	Consistency
Y-Roc	Consist	7	5	7	7	7	7
Finny Fin	Paceset	8	8	4	5	7	8
Neat-O	Clutch	6	5	9	9	6	5
Zick	Round Winner	8	8	7	8	7	7
Jimmy	Clutch	7	8	4	8	5	7
Rox-it	Consist	8	8	6	6	7	7
One	Bomb	8	8	10	8	5	4

Things start to get messy in a crew v. crew, as there are many different orders that you can use with the members of the squad. Generally though, you should have an idea of how to use the members based upon the first few examples.

In this scenario, we've added Jimmy (Clutch), Rox-it (Consistent Bboy) and One (Bomb). Jimmy would come in handy securing a round, and we'd use him towards the middle or end of the battle. Rox-it is a Consistent Bboy and would be useful in the middle of a battle. One fills the role of the Bomb in the crew, and can be used anywhere we'd want to blow shit up. We'd use the Bomb in this case if we were losing badly and needed to drastically change the flow of battle, or on the other end of the spectrum, we were winning and needed to demoralize our enemy.

Remember that the above examples are only so that you can understand the rationale behind making informed decisions about who to assign to what role, and when to send people. Strategy in battle should not be a mistake, and you can greatly change the flow of battle based upon how you and your crew strategize. If you work with your crew effectively, you won't have to fear the outcome of any battle.

Also remember that the above examples only account for your crew. When in a real battle situation, the opponent also has the capacity to change the flow of battle—this is why there is flexibility in your squad, based upon how you need to respond. If one of your crewmembers matches well against the opponent and can beat them, you should send them out to accomplish the task.

UNDERSTANDING WHY WE DETERMINE THE ORDER

You should determine the order based upon the strengths of the dancers that comprise your squad. Generally speaking, you want to use the crewmembers that are consistent and have good style towards the beginning of the battle, and use ones that have strong power and tricks towards the middle and end of the battle.

Often times, we as bboys/bgirls do this intuitively. You have the sense that you want to send dancers with good style out to "warm up" the battle, and then move into more heavy-hitting dancers as the battle progresses. If you stop and think for a moment though, why do we do this? This is something most Floor Generals do, but can they articulate why they do so?

The answer is control. Dancers with better style, floorwork, and musicality tend to have stronger control and more consistency than dancers who rely mainly on physical moves. By sending out a strong dancer first to set the pace, you'll tell both the judges and the crowd: "My crew is in control. My crew is strong. We have more control than our opponent." Conversely, if you send out a dancer strong in power or tricks who tries to blow shit up, even if they hit their moves, they don't scream "control" in the same way. Use a stylish Pacesetter effectively and consider that you have a first impression to make each and every battle. If your Pacesetter comes out with good style in later rounds, you'll send the message in top 16, top 8, top 4, and even the finals that "Yes, we are still in control."

Once your crew has established and maintained control, it won't matter as much if you send out a bboy/bgirl whose style is not as good. At that point in the battle, you'll already control the flow, and you can leave the power/trick bboy/bgirl at ease to hit their moves without having to think (as much) about packaging.

When determining the order of your squad, always play to your crewmembers' strength.

ON WHY TO SEND A STRONG DANCER FIRST

As I mentioned above you would send a strong dancer out first to make a good impression and demonstrate control. Consider the construction of a basic set. Unless you're countering an opponent, you'd start with toprock. Think of the battle as the same type of narrative with a single set, just on a larger scale—your first bboy/bgirl is going to start your first set with toprock. It makes sense to send out the person with the strongest style to showcase how high level your narrative is as a whole.

Generally speaking, bboys/bgirls who rely on style are more consistent in the quality of their sets than bboys/bgirls who rely on moves (again, a generalization, but try to understand the spirit of what I'm saying). These bboys/bgirls will rely on movement more than moves. Even if these bboys/bgirls are running low on moves or patterns, because they move well and interpret music well, they'll be able to make a good impression and set the pace of battle.

WHEN TO USE POWER FIRST

Typically you want to send out someone with strong style first to establish control in the battle. Occasionally though, it is acceptable to start a battle with power, blow ups, or tricks. Of course, if you or your squad are limited to powermoves, you'll want to highlight your strength. The other instance you'd want to start with power is to intimidate or trump your opponent. If you are in a situation where you need to throw something strong to start the battle, and you feel pacing with style isn't going to be enough, or if you know that your opponent will want to use a move that you can eliminate with one of yours, it is acceptable to start with power.

However, I must say that it is risky to start with power because you must execute. It is extremely difficult to recover in a battle if you mess up first round, and even if you execute your power, you need to demonstrate your control throughout. If you do start with power, don't end your round quickly. A round that is too short will make you seem as if you needed to get in and out fast, and it will make you appear uncontrolled.

ON FLOW IN THE MIDDLE ROUNDS

Every part of a battle is important, but in battles that go more than three rounds, a certain flow begins to develop between the opposing crews. Much like the ebb and flow of a body of water, crew battles can change in tempo and ferocity. Typically, Consistent Bboys/Bgirls and Roundwinner Bboys/Bgirls do well to maintain or commandeer the flow of battles towards the middle, but the most important thing is to understand how the battle is flowing while you're in it. Know to change the rhythm of the battle if you feel you are losing. If a rhythm develops that you feel is negative, do something dramatic to disrupt it. Because of the number of rounds, the middle is where you will win or lose in longer battles.

WHY YOU MUST FINISH STRONG

In the same way that I mentioned battles follow the same narrative structure as a set, you'll always want to finish strong—or at least clean and comprehensively. It may seem intuitive, but it must be articulated—the end of your battle will leave a final impression on the judges and the crowd. If you finish strong in a battle you can seal the deal. If you are shaky, you may call the rest of your dancing into question. Finish strong no matter what—even if you mess up, you should not walk out of your set until you finish.

Finishing strong is important not just in rounds and battles and in general, but it takes on particular importance in certain formats. While the final round is more of a punctuation mark in crew battles, in 1v1s of three or more rounds, 2v2s of three or more rounds, or 3v3s that go three rounds (but not more in this case), you must finish strong. This has to do not only with the "complete and comprehensive" idea I mentioned above, but demonstrating your control and versatility in all situations. If you can finish a three round battle in a 1v1 with strength and energy, everyone will perceive you as being in control (whether or not you can go more rounds, you must show and pretend that you can). The same holds true for a 2v2 of four rounds—you can't show any signs of waning energy, and by ending strong, you give the impression that you can continue battling. In a 3v3, the first and third rounds tend to hold more weight. Judges will often go into the third round thinking "Well, it's tied one to one," and will give equal weight to the first two rounds, making a determination from the third round.

ON BEING A FLOOR GENERAL

Being a Floor General is difficult. Occasionally, crews will assign the responsibility of the Floor General to someone who is not actually in the battle, or simply not have one. While the former is acceptable, it is unacceptable not to have a Floor General in your squad—this will lead to disorganization, a lack of proper pacing in your battle, and your squad will look unprepared. It is better to have a bad Floor General than none at all.

As Floor General you must be decisive. Even if your pacing isn't perfect and you don't always make perfect decisions, that is alright—the important thing is to give off the appearance that your crew is organized and is acting with intention (your Tatemae). The more experienced you become and the more you study, the more you'll become effective at commanding your squad.

With that said, being a Floor General comes naturally to some, and is difficult for others—no matter your starting point, you can learn to be an effective Floor General. The most important things are preparing for the battle, having a firm grasp of general strategy, knowing the nuances of your squad, and keeping calm. Be sure to communicate with your squad before, during and after the battle. Make sure everyone is on the same page.

One of the most difficult aspects of being a Floor General is understanding the flow of the battle while you are in it. You must learn to evaluate your crew's rounds as objectively as possible— this will help you make good decisions and control the battle more effectively. It can be difficult to actually throw a round, feel the flow of the battle, and still make good decisions. With practice you'll be able to juggle these different aspects of battle. Preparation and practice are key.

ON DIFFERENT BATTLE FORMATS

In this section, I'll discuss the different battle formats in terms of the size of the crew. I will not discuss concept formats such as the "win your round" format employed at the Stylelements Anniversary

Jams, "Jack of All Trades" that Dyno Rock hosts, or R-16 and Kozen style systems. I'll leave those to your discretion for now.

Know that while the general principles of a good round and good battle strategy hold true no matter the format of the battle, there are distinctly different things happening in each format of a battle. If you're unsure of what to do, stick to the general principles of what it means to do good rounds.

1V1S

1v1s are short. They are hard to get a flow for, and they tend to favor more well-rounded, complete dancers. Dancers who are more consistent and have their sense of personality well developed tend to do better in 1v1s. These are also difficult because you can't rely on your crew if you aren't on point. Conversely, many bboys/bgirls like 1v1s because there is no pressure from your crew to perform—you are there to battle for yourself.

One Round – You must win this round. You must control yourself and all other variables. Outperform your opponent and leave no questions. Keep control of the pacing of your set—since there will be two rounds (including your opponent's) the actual flow of your set controls the battle.

Two Rounds – Your second round is weighted slightly more than your first round. It is acceptable to start your first round slowly, but if you start your second round at a slow tempo, you'll appear tired. Do a complete first round, and blow your opponent out your second round.

If you're facing an opponent you truly feel you can't beat, try your best to do a solid first round, and stake everything on your second round. If you're lucky, they'll be tired and do a mediocre round. If you blow them out in the second round, you may force a tie-breaker that you can win, or simply take the battle by virtue of the second round. Consider the strength of your opponent and act accordingly.

Three Rounds – In a three round 1v1, your first and third rounds are weighted more than your second round, with slightly more weight given to the third round. Execute a heavy first round, use the second round to exhibit control and completion, and do a hard powermove or blowup in your third round. No matter what, be energetic in your third round. Unless you're competing in Red Bull BC One or another high level jam, the fact that you're in a three round 1v1 probably means you're in the finals or semi-finals—if this is the case, both you and your opponent will be low on hard moves. Win with energy and strategy.

More Than Four Rounds – The middle is important for a 1v1 of more than four rounds, but your 5th round will be heavily weighted as well. A battle of four or more rounds is long enough to develop a sense of flow, so use your general sense of strategy to win the battle through the flow of the middle rounds. Again, you must keep your energy high and win with your energy in the latter rounds. Having energy in your last round when your opponent is visibly tired will give you a huge advantage.

2V2S

2v2s are also a short battle format, but you're allowed a bit more of an exchange with your opponents. There can be changes in the flow of the battle even in this small space, and variables can arise and go wrong. As mentioned before, you want to play to the strengths of yourself and your crewmate.

One Round Each – Generally speaking, you should assign a Pacesetter and a Clutch (or switch either for a Consistent Bboy/

Bgirl) whether or not you have to slightly bend the definitions of the roles. Place the person with better style at the start of the battle to form the start of your "set," and place the person with strong "moves" in the second spot.

Two or More Rounds Each – Your tactics should not change too much in this situation. Typically, you'll put the person with better style in as the Pacesetter and place the person with stronger moves as the Clutch. When your battles go four or more rounds in a 2v2 situation, you'll want to be sure that you finish strong. In the case that The Clutch has one strong round and one mediocre round at their disposal, they should do the mediocre round first (i.e. the 2nd round of the battle) and finish with the stronger round (4th/final round of the battle). Finishing strong will create the perception that you have energy and can continue dancing.

The Pacesetter's job is just as important in the third (or fifth) round in an extended battle situation. While the Pacesetter typically sets the tone of the battle in the first round, their job is to commandeer the flow of the battle in the third or fifth round. Much as they would do in the first round, they can do this by exhibiting control—they can change tempo, stay on top longer, or generally draw attention to the flaws of their opponents. Because they'll be operating in the middle of the battle, there won't be as much pressure to finish strong, and they can focus on manipulating the pace/flow of the battle.

When to Change Your Order – Again, you should generally keep the person with better style in the front position in 2v2s. Sometimes, though, it can become necessary to change the positions because you match particularly well against your opponents. More often than not, you'll change the order of attack when you're responding to your opponents—if you're going first, always send the person with better style first. If, however, changing the order in response to your opponent will allow you to commandeer the flow of the battle or put you in a situation to more effectively win both rounds, you should do so.

Three Rounds Each Side – Occasionally you'll get put into a situation when each side has to do three rounds—usually the promotor of the jam will do this to help exhibit the strength, versatility, and endurance of the crews involved. Three round battles are much different, because one of the two bboys/bgirls will have to go twice. Much the same as a 2v2 that goes four or more rounds you must finish strong. You must also consider where in the jam this is happening—consider your opponent, and if you're facing them in top 16, top 8, or top 4.

Generally speaking, if you're facing a weak opponent, use the person with less endurance in the earlier round (to save the stronger bboy/bgirl for a possible three round battle later). If you're facing a strong opponent and you're in a must-win situation, use the stronger bboy/bgirl twice. Consider that if you use the stronger bboy/bgirl to get past top 16 and didn't necessarily need to, the weaker of the two may have to face a (likely) stronger opponent in top 8. If both bboys/bgirls are of similar level and strength that day, consider who matches better to your opponent and the working conditions, and decide from there.

3V3S

3v3s begin to become full conversations, even if you're only doing one round per bboy/bgirl. You can have distinctive styles on each side, respond and converse with your opponent, and the battle is long enough for a flow to develop and change. As with any other format of a battle, you must play to the strengths of the bboys/bgirls on your squad. In 3v3s and above, the distinct roles of each bboy/bgirl begin to become more evident—rather than just having a Pacesetter and a Clutch as in a 2v2, you can have any number of roles in a 3v3 and mix and match them.

Generally speaking, the rules of pacing a 3v3 are the same as pacing a 1v1 or 2v2 that goes three rounds—start exhibiting control and take the pace of the battle. The second round can be dedicated to flow, and the last round tends to have more weight. As a result, you should put someone with strong moves and execution in the 3rd position. If you've got a Bomb on your squad, you might do better to put them in the 2nd position—if they execute, you'll have commandeered the flow of the battle and it will be too far gone in your direction for your opponent to recover. If they mess up, your 3rd bboy/bgirl should be able to execute and draw attention away from the mess-up.

If 3v3s go two or more rounds per person, they should be paced as crew battles. Because there are so many rounds, the middle is where the battle is won and lost—pay particular attention to how the battle is flowing, how you're responding to the opponent, and how the variables are responding to you. If the flow is not going well, you can switch up tactics, and change positions. You should have enough time to recover between rounds, so if you need to swap the order of attack, you can do so in the second round.

4V4S

4v4s are the start of what can be considered a "crew battle." Much in the same way that a 3v3 allows for complexity and specific roles, so does a 4v4. The challenge that 4v4s often pose is building a squad so strong that there aren't any weak points. 2v2s and 3v3s are niche enough that they tend to allow you to build a squad without any weak bboys/bgirls. The very fact of building a 4v4 squad with four strong bboys/bgirls can be difficult. While I believe that you can sometimes get away with one or two weak bboys/bgirls in larger crew battles (five or more), if you can assemble a squad of four solid bboys/bgirls, you'll do well. Your style, pacing, and execution will be weighted more heavily in this situation because you can commandeer flow and take middle rounds. Try to build a squad with similar skill levels and consistency in theme—if you can demonstrate your "crewnity" (crew unity), that will go farther than raw skill.

Again, pay attention to the middle rounds in this situation. Always start with a Pacesetter, always end strong.

You can have more flexibility to play with in the second and third rounds—whatever you do, be intentional about your strategy. Exhibit your strengths and draw attention to your opponent's flaws.

OTHER CREW BATTLES (FIVE AND MORE)

Crew battles of five or more can be a true dialogue. As mentioned in the formats above, you'll be able to converse in even greater depth with the other crew. Judges and the crowd tend to value this exchange and your responses in this format. While the specific roles that your crewmembers play is important, you'll have to pay attention to both the Forest and the Trees—be smart about the bboys/bgirls that you send out, when you use them, and consider how this will change the flow of a battle.

If you've only got one bboy/bgirl on your squad with power or tricks, use them as a response. Consider a crew battle where your squad has strong style but not lots of blow-ups. If you use them first, your opponent will probably respond with good power or tricks—you're then left to use style as a response. This is not a negative thing in and of itself, but you lose the choice of how to respond. This may be perceived as a weakness—you'll have to work extra hard to convince the crowd and judges that you don't have a deficit.

On the other hand, if you can respond with power or tricks, you then have the option of how to respond in the following round— you can demonstrate that you have power and tricks, but also other forms of control. Consider how you'll be perceived when choosing the order of attack. Show no weaknesses.

ON JUDGING AND OTHER FORMATS

On Timed Battles – Timed battles can take extra effort from certain bboys/bgirls and the Floor General. Consider that you're going to get roughly one round per minute (sometimes more, sometimes less) and plan accordingly.

If in a 2v2, you're fine to stick with your original plan and just make sure that you finish strong no matter whose round you land on—try to save a strong round for when you hear the MC say "last round."

In a 3v3, you may have enough flexibility to choose who goes last— use the Pacesetter first and pay attention to the flow in the middle of the battle. Finish strong in response to the call for "last round."

As in smaller formats as well, in a 4v4 you're still obligated to try to have each bboy/bgirl go out equitably (it will become obvious if you don't). You'll have enough flexibility to change the order of attack mid-battle, but you'll be marked down if one of your squad members is visibly tired. Consider this and plan accordingly.

In a 5v5 or greater, you'll have the flexibility to hide weaker bboys/bgirls if you don't necessarily want to send them out. Consider when you can best exhibit their strengths and send them out at that point in the battle. Your stronger bboys/bgirls can eat up the brunt of the time in these situations. Maintain strong strategy.

On Prelims – Prelims can be a difficult barrier to overcome. As a starting bboy/bgirl, getting past prelims and into an actual battle can be very difficult. Even as an experienced bboy/bgirl, there are some situations where you'll be in a new scene or with new judges and you may be judged by your perceived "rep"—as a result, it can be difficult to pass prelims in a new or unfamiliar scene. You're also battling in a sense of unknown—typically prelims aren't "win your battle," so it can be difficult to gauge how much you should do.

There are two perspectives you must understand when approaching prelims and battles in general—competent judges and incompetent judges.

The Perspective of Competent Judges – Competent judges will be looking at your general level of skill, how you move and package things, if you execute, and if you demonstrate anything unique. Of course, they'll also be paying attention to your musicality and your general battle strategy. For the purpose of prelims, you should demonstrate your ability to comfortably utilize your weapons and your unique personality as a dancer.

In other words, I reject the idea that you should change how you dance based upon what you think the judges will want—if someone with good footwork is judging, people often want to do more footwork, thinking the judge will look more favorably upon it. If someone with good power is judging, people will want to try to do more power or tricks. This is faulty because if a bboy/bgirl is skilled in any of those areas, they'll likely judge more harshly and notice flaws because they are good at those things.

Again, you should be as true to yourself as possible—you'll dance better if you like what you're doing, and this will reflect in your performance. Competent judges will see this—they'll notice the intangible things that you are doing in your dance, rather than how much of an automaton you are.

The Perspective of Incompetent Judges – For incompetent judges, your sets will blur together with the rest of the crowd. Incompetent judges will judge based solely upon inconsequential things—if they liked a particular dancer's shorts, if they had a conversation with a dancer beforehand, if they look at a dancer and "know that they can do better" even if they didn't execute. These tend to be the types of judges that will let people with a rep through, even if they do wack sets in prelims. It is unfortunate to say, but these types of judges abound—they won't judge based upon what people do in their prelim sets, but the rep of those battling.

If you have a panel of incompetent judges in a field where you might actually blend in with the rest of the crowd, you have to throw strong material. Do something a little bit shocking, hit a beat in a different way, throw a unique powermove, or just generally blow the crowd up.

Because incompetent judges won't be paying attention to you, you have to wake them up—do something to stand out. Make it so that they have no choice but to put you through past prelims.

In reality, most judges are probably going to fall somewhere in the middle, and you should probably be coming from a place of neutrality when deciding what to do. Assume the judges might be incompetent (unless you know otherwise), but dance for them as if they would understand what you're doing like a competent judge. Use your own judgement in this case, but always dance like yourself.

On Short Timed Prelims – Short timed prelims usually happen in crew battles at large events. These can be unfortunate situations when the girth of the field makes it such that you can only use a few bboys/bgirls in a crew battle. If this is the case, you must do whatever you can to demonstrate that you should get through to the battle round. In other words, blow shit up...with a condition. Blow shit up, but don't be mindless about it. Choose the bboys/bgirls that best exhibit the spirit of your crew and send them out in a fury.

One of the hardest prelim rounds I've seen came from Extraordinary Gentlemen (EXG) at Freestyle Session (FSS) 12. Not only did they throw some of their best material, but the way they paced the battle and who they attacked with showcased their crew spirit accurately.

A common pitfall of timed prelims is forgetting that you must exhibit your spirit as a crew—people just try to blow shit up. Balance and execution in the midst of expression and blowing shit up is the key here.

On Showcase Prelims – Some event organizers and judges tend to prefer to do showcase prelims rather than battle prelims (i.e. an entire crew goes out and does performance rounds in succession, rather than "battling" another crew for prelims). These type of prelims are faulty to begin with—you don't get an accurate feel for the field because you don't see how they respond in battles. Regardless, some organizers still use showcases because they think it will save them time or they don't know any better. In these cases, be prepared and know what to do.

The number one question bboys/bgirls have about showcase prelims is where to direct their energy. Consider this—showcase prelims are set up as a performance, not a battle. As a result, bboys/bgirls are often thrown off because they'll feel like they are performing and their energy and execution will suffer.

When doing a showcase prelim, you can create a battle scenario. The most common way to do this is to battle the judges. If you pretend that you are in a battle with the judges this will completely change your energy, and the judges will perceive that you are ready to be in a real battle setting. Additionally, this will give you focus, help your execution, and generally help the perception of your crew in this situation.

ON CYPHER PRELIMS

If you like dancing in cypher prelims and feel that you do well in the medium, I encourage you to pursue and battle at them as much as you can—if you feel they showcase your strengths, then you should attack this as much as possible. As a rule though, I avoid battling at jams that use cypher prelims.

Cypher prelims can be good for bboys/bgirls because there are more elements that you can control—you can control how many times you go out, you can more easily control which songs you dance to, and you can burn through as many or as few moves as you'd like because you can more rely on vibing and working with the energy of the cypher as opposed to a structured battle.

I dislike cypher prelims, however, because there are too many variables. Judges tend to have a harder time objectively choosing who will get past prelims because there is so much happening in such a short amount of time—they also don't always know the names of the bboys/bgirls in the cypher, so they'll tend to choose bboys/bgirls they know. If someone does stand out to them, they tend to go by "feel" rather than the quality of the bboy/bgirl's sets—for a competition, this becomes problematic. Additionally, judges are either expected to walk among cyphers, or watch a single cypher (in the case that there are multiple cyphers) and this makes it difficult for them to accurately and fairly judge.

Beyond the difficult judging system, the very fact of the cypher itself becomes difficult to dance in. Since the bboys/bgirls involved in the prelim will be looking for floor time, you'll struggle to actually get on the floor. With five or six bboys/bgirls rushing to get floor time, it can be both difficult and dangerous. Sadly, in cypher prelims, the decorum of cyphering is often cast aside as bboys/bgirls will think that more floor time will guarantee them a better chance of getting past prelims.

I have to emphasize that if you like cypher prelims and do well in them, I encourage you to pursue battling at jams with cypher prelims. I do, however, want to draw attention to the fact that you'll have to overcome more variables in such a style of battling than you would at other events. Be aware of the positives and negatives of such a medium.

GENERAL STRATEGY

UNDERSTANDING THE SPACE

Different jams will put you in different spatial situations—you must understand how to respond in each of these. I've gone into a greater discussion of how space can affect your dancing and your energy in the Earth book, but know that these will manifest at jams.

Rather than going into a catalog discussion of the different situations you'll find yourself in, know that you must contend with warming up and possibly cyphering in harsh situations, and then battling in similar conditions. Pay particular attention to the placement of the judges and how they'll perceive your moves and the angles. Check the placement of the DJ and if they can see you to make educated decisions on when to switch the music. See if any of your sides are to a wall, if there are props you or other bboys/ bgirls might play with (pipes, roofing, a basketball hoop) and how the crowd is set up. Pay attention to your environment and plan accordingly.

ON NOT SUCCUMBING TO
THE SURROUNDING ENERGY OF A JAM

This idea is similar to understanding the space, but different because it has to do with people's energy. While the space is the physical environment, the bboys/bgirls, spectators, music, and all other things will contribute the energy of a jam. Especially at jams that are focused on battling or have higher level bboys/bgirls, there will be a lot of nervous tension—this is because most of the other dancers aren't considering what they are doing with their energy, and may be dispersing it throughout the environment. People may be tense, dancing too fast, and hype to the point of being uncontrolled. Again, consider the analogy I gave earlier of being a swimmer at sea—stay in control and you won't risk drowning. Move at your own pace, control your energy, and keep your head above water.

UNDERSTANDING HOW YOUR SET
AFFECTS THE OPPONENT

Since battles are a conversation, depending on what you do in your round, you'll elicit a response from your opponent. In situations like these, it is very important to know your enemy—depending on what you know about your opponent, you'll be able to gauge what their reaction will be, and much like a game of chess, you can control the outcome of the battle as well.

On a basic level, if you throw a high level set that your opponent has no chance of beating, you can scare them into submission. If you're facing a higher level opponent and do a strong set, they'll want to respond with a high level set as well—whether or not you win, you'll probably have a good exchange, and this is often more important than just winning a jam.

Consider other possibilities though. If your opponent commandeers the flow of a battle and completely blows shit up, the ball is then in your court—you could respond with Fire and gamble to try to steal the flow of the battle, but then you run the risk that they'll maintain the flow. On the other hand, you could do a slower, more controlled set that is still good, just don't blow shit up. By pacing down the battle, you'll stop their flow, and throw off what they're doing in subsequent rounds. Naturally though, this won't work to win a one round battle as you'll need to win the single round—this can be done in longer battles.

Other possibilities have to do with giving your opponent (and responding with) different elements and considering how these will affect your opponent. Try to maintain the element of surprise—as much as you can, avoid being predictable. Keep your opponent guessing and try to throw them off balance in an intentional way.

ON BEATING YOUR OPPONENT'S ROUNDS

It seems obvious to say this, but to win a battle you must beat your opponent's round. Often though, you will "beat" your opponent's rounds and not win a battle—this is a matter of perception. Of course, when you enter a bboy/bgirl jam you're subject to the whims of the judges—if the judges don't like you, don't like your style, aren't paying attention, or are incompetent, you may lose. Your job is to destroy your opponent so thoroughly that there is absolutely no question in anyone's mind that you've won the battle. Unless you're limited on moves and stamina, you should approach every jam with this mentality—don't underestimate any opponent and try to convince the judges beyond a doubt that you've won.

Of course, this isn't always realistic, so you've got to find ways to beat your opponent without always having the option to completely destroy them. Typically, the most effective way to do so when you can't soundly beat them is to "edge them out." To edge out your opponent means to beat them clearly but not by a huge margin. Edging out your opponent can be dangerous because the judges might not agree with the fact that you've won the battle. If you don't have any options, this is the thing to do. You may be in different situations for this:

Going First – Edging out your opponent is hard to do when you're going first since you can't gauge what they've done. In this case, you simply have to dance your dance and try your best to put them in a bad situation with the song, or dance strongly enough to show deficits on their end. The advantage to this is that you set the pace—you set the bar and can intimidate with your set. Focus on executing your style; in these situations you have the autonomy to do what you want and not have to make decisions in response. You can simply battle.

Going Second (Responding) – Edging out your opponent is easier when responding, but you have to think quickly and execute. It's easier to gauge how to do this, but harder to execute than going first. You have the benefit of seeing your opponent's set and knowing how much you need to do to beat them. The difficult part comes with the fact of having to respond, being at the whim of your opponent's timing, the part of the song you get, and how the crowd responds to you. Pay attention to what your opponent is doing and how strong of a set you'll need to throw. If you're going second, always do a round slightly harder than you would think you'd need to edge them out.

CREWNITY & CHEMISTRY: WHY "CREW" VERSUS "SQUAD" MATTERS

While creating a Super Crew—or a squad from multiple crews— can be extremely powerful and often win jams, there are definite benefits to maintaining the same members of a crew versus creating a squad from multiple crews. While the raw talent of a squad may be extremely high, it will often be evident to the audience and judges that they are indeed an assemblage of different parts and don't have a common theme. Because of this, people may often mark the squad down, or look less favorably upon them.

On the other hand, a squad made of members from the same crew will generally have an intangible power amongst them that makes them stronger as a team. Since the crew will have been practicing and spending time together, as well as have battle experience together, they'll naturally understand each other's ebbs and flows, nuances on and off the floor, and know how to work well with each other.

Even in battles where the bboys/bgirls only do solo rounds, all this will manifest itself as "chemistry," and the crew will appear to have a theme running through their rounds—both the crowd and the judges will look favorably upon the fact that you've built upon one another.

Additionally, knowing the strengths and weaknesses of your fellow crewmembers can help each solo bboy/bgirl understand when to do stronger rounds, when to hold back, and when to showcase or support the other members. Although hard to measure in tangible terms, the chemistry that comes with a "crew" versus a "squad" will become evident to the viewer.

ON SACRIFICING ROUNDS (USE SPARINGLY)

Sacrificing rounds is a tactic that you should understand, know how to do, but use sparingly. By purposely gambling or losing a round, you can in turn win an entire battle, but you do so at a risk.

Consider a three round bboy/bgirl battle. Suppose you're facing a crew with one extremely strong bboy/bgirl (who no one on your squad can beat, let's rate them at a "10" out of 10), and two mediocre bboys/bgirls—let's say they're both valued at "5" out of 10. Also consider that at your disposal you have two solid bboys/bgirls—let's say "7's"—and one mediocre bboy/bgirl—a "5". For a visual, it'll look like this:

	1st Round Bboy/Bgirl	2nd Round Bboy/Bgirl	3rd Round Bboy/Bgirl
Your Squad	7	7	5
Their Squad	10	5	5

In this scenario, you'll send one of your solid bboys/bgirls, a "7" against their "10," hoping for a win or at least a solid showing...of course, you'll lose. You may win your second round, but then you risk losing your third round by having the two mediocre bboys/bgirls battle. You might also consider that the judges would look favorably on the team with the strongest bboy/bgirl.

Consider, though, if you were to change the order:

	1st Round Bboy/Bgirl	2nd Round Bboy/Bgirl	3rd Round Bboy/Bgirl
Your Squad	5	7	7
Their Squad	10	5	5

Now, this is not a foolproof plan—this is why I say to use this tactic only in certain occasions. However, if you look above, you'll have won the battle two rounds to one round, against a squad with a possibly superior bboy/bgirl. By changing the order of attack, and purposely using your mediocre bboy/bgirl against their stronger bboy/bgirl, you could potentially win the battle.

Why This Can Be a Risky Strategy – Although in the above scenario you may have won the rounds, sometimes you'll have lost the first round so badly, that you'll be unable to recover and the judges will dismiss your squad. Much in the same way, if your "5" faced their "10" in the third round, even if you were winning the battle up until that point, your "5" may get so crushed that it will call the rest of the battle into question. If you're purposely throwing a round, know that you or your crewmember must do a good enough round to keep you in the game—you might lose the round, but at least try to make a good showing.

On Creating Ties by Sacrificing Rounds – Again, this is not a foolproof strategy because it depends on the judges, but you can sometimes create ties by throwing a round, much in the same way as above. Consider a 2v2 or a 1v1 with two rounds. If your opponent throws a crazy round that you know you can't beat, do a solid round in response, but put all your effort into beating their second round. If you can do this and wear them down, you may create a situation where you'll force a tie-breaker, and you could potentially win that. Rather than throwing all your moves against their first hard round and risk losing, know that you can sacrifice that round, and win later. I have to state once more that this is not foolproof, but is something that can work in extraneous circumstances.

ON ETIQUETTE IN BATTLES

Etiquette in battles is important not only for the sake of the battle at hand, but because of the bigger picture of your bboy/bgirl career. While it is important to do as well as you can and do your best to win battles, you also want to consider the persona that you're creating for yourself in the bboy/bgirl scene. By breaking the rules of etiquette, you'll be marketing yourself as one that doesn't want to play by the rules—this will make it harder for you to get invited to battles, do well in some judges' eyes, win jams, and make allies.

Now, I do agree that you should break the rules of bboying/bgirling if you'd like to—dance differently, present yourself differently, and build your own persona. You should still, however, maintain the rules of decorum—have a good attitude, don't start fights or touch your opponents, and win or lose respectfully. Even if you disagree with a judge's decision, you can call them out in a respectful way— generally, play by the rules of battle and have a good attitude, and people will respect you for it. If you choose to break a rule, do so with intention, and don't do anything that would be destructive or harmful to others. Everyone deserves your respect.

ON BURNS

Burns are physical gestures that are meant to embarrass your opponent, such as a cock gesture, shooting your opponent, or pretending to cut off their head. I'm not going to go into huge detail about burns or catalog the ways to approach them, but burns are important enough that I want to discuss them conceptually. Burns are a way that you can upset your opponent's rhythm, and provoke them into falling into your strategy. Generally speaking, burns are a way to take advantage of your opponent's openings and showcase their weakness.

While there are no definite rules regarding burns, you should know that by putting yourself in close contact with your opponent, you create risk. When you do burns, you should strike fast, and don't dwell too long. Whatever burns you choose to employ, know that these are meant to make you appear in control, and make your opponent look foolish.

ON TRASH TALKING

While burns are physical gestures meant to show dominance over your opponent, I want to discuss trash talking as a verbal tactic. Trash talking is a tactic that many bboys/bgirls employ to get into their opponents' heads. Trash talking can be effective in the heat of the moment, but you can be perceived as crass and distasteful—with that said, competitive displays such as battles can become aggressive, and you should expect that many people will trash talk against you. Generally, I agree with gesturing in battle—shrug if your opponent's round is mediocre, show signs of distaste on your face, or wag your finger at an opponent. These are ways of showing that you are engaged in a battle.

Going out of your way to verbally abuse an opponent in battle, however, can be destructive. If you talk too much or are too disrespectful, the crowd, judges, and your opponents will look down upon you for this. People may also look at what you are doing and fail to perceive it as a battle tactic—they will equate your trash talking with your out-of-battle persona, and this can be destructive for your overall place in the scene.

As a rule, trash talking is acceptable, but I encourage you to keep it tasteful. I disagree with the notion that you should only win with moves—energy, packaging, pacing, and angles of attack will win you battles in conjunction with the strength of your moves. Much in the same way that you shouldn't rely on the moves themselves to win you battles, you can't rely on your mouth. Whatever you do, do with intention and an understanding of how you will be perceived.

When your opponent is talking trash against you, it is not appropriate to respond—by responding to their trash talking, you'll show that you are giving in to their game, and what they are doing is affecting you. Understand that they are trying to get into your head, keep your cool, and execute. You'll be perceived favorably if you can maintain your cool.

ON STEALING ROUNDS

Generally speaking, stealing rounds is not acceptable in an organized competition. Unless the host of the event expressly says that you may steal rounds, I'd advise against doing so.

With that said, coming out aggressively and making sure your opponent does not have the time to counter can be an effective way to steal the momentum of a battle—when you do this, you must wait for a break in the opponent's set. They may get up and look confused, end their round, or show a moment of weakness— you should strike in this instant. An excellent example of someone stealing a round in an effective and respectful way was Lil' Ceng in the top 16 round of the Redbull BC One World Finals in 2008. Rather than dwelling on the point, he simply started his set strongly and decisively, and didn't give his opponent the opportunity to respond. Strike quickly if you decide that this is a tactic that you'd like to employ.

ON TIE-BREAKERS

Understand that tie-breakers aren't necessarily just an extra round tacked onto a battle. This is the judges' way of gauging where the two crews are in the moment, and who can draw up greater strength. Generally, tie-breakers happen because the judges aren't convinced that there was a decisive winner to the battle. They need to see not just who will "win" the next round, but who can demonstrate that they have the fire to keep moving forward in the jam, who still has energy reserves, and who still has moves left.

Of course, try to win your round, but be sure to do so with energy, decisiveness, and by showing a variety to your arsenal. Tie-breakers are rarely won simply because of a good set, but rather because of a matter of momentum.

When given the opportunity to do a tie-breaker in the finals, you must understand that your opponent is working in their reserves of energy and moves as well—if you're in a tie-breaker in the finals, you'll both probably have nearly maxed out. Keep your cool, pick a decisive move, and perform your set with energy and intention.

I want to again emphasize the fact that routines are unacceptable in tie-breakers. Unless the MC, host, or judges specifically call for routines in your tie-breaker, you should not be doing them.

ON CRASHING IN BATTLES

Crashing in battles is not only very destructive to the flow of your set, but will likely put you in a "fight or flight" mental state. While the judges may look at your crash very harshly, you must understand that sometimes you may crash—be prepared for this instant if it does happen and know that the battle is not yet over. You can still win. The important thing to know when you crash in a battle is not to show that you are upset or acknowledge the crash—you must do your best to play it off. If you appear confident in your crash and finish your set strongly, you'll at least stay in the battle. However, if you acknowledge the crash, appear down on yourself, or walk out of your set, you'll definitely have lost the battle. If you can make a crash appear like it didn't phase you, you'll be able to convince onlookers that you haven't lost yet.

Hong-10 is one of the best bboys to watch recover from crashes—his moves are so high risk-high reward that crashes are inevitable. When he does crash, he does not dwell on the crash, but continues charging onward and finishes his set as if the entire series of moves was intentional.

ON RESPONDING TO DIFFERENT ROUNDS

A Wack Round – You should get to the level where you should never be in danger of losing to a wack round. Assuming that you are at the level where you will not lose to a wack round, you must consider how to appropriately respond. This is one of the few times it is acceptable to give energy to your opponent. Typically the person throwing a wack round at you will be a beginner—rather than demoralizing them or talking trash, it is ok to encourage them, in the hopes that they will do well. Even at their best, they probably still won't be able to beat you. They (and the crowd and judges) will remember your positive attitude and you'll have made an ally. In your set, do something solid—you want to show that you're taking them seriously (although there is no need to absolutely destroy them) and you will be seen as giving your due respect to every person you battle, rather than underestimating anyone. This will be perceived favorably.

A Round at Your Level – When someone does a round at your level, you must beat them by using the "intangible" aspects of bboying/bgirling—you have to display your creativity, beat them by channeling your energy, or execute better than they did. When a round at your level comes at you, you have to do your best to cover all bases to make it clear that you are the superior dancer. Even if the moves are at your level (or perhaps higher level), you can beat your opponent by showcasing your superiority and control in other aspects.

A Round Higher Than Your Level – Even if your opponent does a round with moves at a higher level than you can do, you could still possibly win the round. The important thing here is to make sure that you don't lose composure, and to be sure to keep your round as strong as possible.

You could still convince the judges that you should get through, and quite possibly even force a tie-breaker. In a worst case scenario when an opponent does a round beyond your capacity to beat, if you still throw a solid round and show that you refuse to back down in the face of adversity, people will give you respect—by battling well against strong opponents, you'll be able to increase your rep.

UNDERSTANDING DIRECTION WHEN BATTLING

You should always be intentional about where you direct your energy in battles—you should also be aware of how the angles of your moves and the angles of your energy will affect the way people perceive you.

It is a good thing to focus your energy on your opponent and make eye contact in your moves; however, if you stay facing the same direction for your entire set, you'll appear very one dimensional. You can move your energy from the crowd, your crew, the judges, or even the environment—the important thing is to use the opponent as the main focal point.

Much in the same way that you want to be intentional about where to direct your energy, you should be intentional about where to direct your moves. Consider where the judges are when executing your moves—are there some moves that you do right or left handed that they won't see? If you're doing a thread, will your body block the thread so the judges don't see? Consider placement and the judges, as well as your environment—build a repertoire of moves that look good from any direction, and if you have moves that only look good from a particular angle, understand that weakness and work to overcome it by showcasing the move properly.

WINNING THREE ROUND BATTLES

Although I talked about this in the battle format section above, I believe this is important enough to elicit a section of its own. Especially in 1v1 situations, bboys/bgirls will find themselves in three round battles—typically this is towards the latter rounds of a jam (semi-finals or finals), unless they are at a higher level jam like BC One. The key here is to win the first and the third round.

Judges tend to give the third round more weight—this is a combination of the last set being fresh in the judge's mind at the end of the battle, but they also take this as an indicator of where you are as a whole. You could easily win your first two rounds, but if you self-destruct on your third, you will call the rest of the battle into question.

When you find yourself in a three round battle, it is important to know how to pace your sets—create a valley. That is to say, start with a strong set, put a solid set in the middle, and end with a strong set. You do this for several reasons. First, start with a strong set because you want to display dominance and control from the very beginning of the battle. If you can win your first round (or even tie it), you'll be in a good position. If you completely lose your first round, it will be difficult to recover, so it must be strong. In your second round, you don't want to throw it away, but you don't need to come out guns blazing unless you absolutely have the capability to do a strong third round. Use your second round as a pacer— maintain solid energy, be in control, and execute a good round without anything too crazy. You do this so you can save your energy for a monstrous third round.

By doing a strong third round in a three round battle, you're doing several things—first and on the most basic level, you're winning a round. Beyond that, if you have strong moves and use them in your third round, your opponent and the judges will think that you have more moves to burn through, and will be able to use them in a tie-breaker. Finally, if you can do a strong third round, you will convince your opponent and the judges that you still have energy. If you show that you have stamina, execution, and variety by doing this, you'll win three round battles.

ON GOING FIRST
OR WAITING IN BATTLES

I've discussed the particular aspects of going first or second when talking about how to edge out your opponents. I want to add a few things here to consider when deciding how to approach the order of attack in battles.

Musashi tells us that if you decide to go first, you should "swiftly make the attack with no hesitation. This should be an initial attack which on the surface is very forceful and fast, but leaves you some reserve. Do not spend all your energy on your first attack." Again, Musashi is not telling us that we should always make the first attack, but should we decide to, we should do it with decisiveness. I must also comment that by "forceful and fast," he does not necessarily mean a quick set, but something done with speed and strength.

In addition to going first, you also have the choice to go second—this seems like an obvious statement, but I want to emphasize the fact of choice that you have here. Musashi comments that "when the opponent attacks with force, if you counterattack with an even more forceful attack, the rhythm with which the opponent attacks is altered. Take advantage of that moment of change, and attain victory." I do have to comment that as bboys/bgirls, we don't necessarily have to be "more forceful" in our response—the important thing here is to note the fact of changing the opponent's rhythm. If we can commandeer the pace of a battle by going slower and appearing more in control, this is beneficial. Depending on how we respond, we can create breaks in the opponent's rhythm, and use this to our advantage.

ON ROUTINES/DANCING AS A CREW

My general rule of thumb is that you should not do routines just for the sake of doing routines. By doing routines for the sake of routines, you'll accomplish little more than being generic—you may execute the routine itself, but you won't necessarily benefit as a result. Do routines with a purpose in mind.

On Building Routines – Routines exist to exhibit crewnity. Whether crewnity is in the fact that your squad has extremely strong footwork or toprock, can build towers with your crewmembers and have the confidence to flip off one another, this is arbitrary. The thing that matters is that you have to show something that is a proper representation of your crew as a whole, and routines give you the ability to showcase that. When building and executing routines, you should consider these facts.

On Executing Routines – Routines are ultimately a type of choreography. Different than typical choreography in the dance world, though, we are dancers that are subject to the whim of the DJ. Be smart about when you choose to throw your routines, and understand the songs in battle well enough not to throw a routine when a dead part of the song is coming up—generally you'll need a maintained snare to keep your crew on beat. Also practice to songs of different tempos to make sure that if you get a slow or fast song in a battle, you'll be able to execute the routine effectively.

When throwing routines in a battle, never count "five, six, seven, eight," or wait for the next eight counts to come—this will appear obvious, and it will make you look unorganized, new to dancing, and will generally mark you down enough to make even strong routines useless.

Rather, have a dancer call the routine in their set—they will have a move that will cue the rest of the dancers that "the routine is coming up." Generally, it is good to throw the sign on the "one count," so that the rest of the dancers can set on the "two through eight" counts, and you'll start the routine on the one. Rather than waiting, the dancer who called the routine can throw the sign, continue dancing, and everyone will transition into the routine on the one without an obvious break.

If someone in your squad messes up, they must continue the routine at the parts they remember and dance to the best of their ability. Whatever you and your crew do (even in your mess ups), it must appear intentional. Don't be predictable, and never give anything away.

WHEN IT IS APPROPRIATE TO DO ROUTINES

In a Battle – It is appropriate to do routines to start a battle, or towards the early to middle stages. This is to set a precedent of how strong your crew is, and how strong your crewnity is. If in a crew battle or extended timed battle, it is a good idea to throw a routine towards the middle to try to commandeer the flow. Generally, if you throw a routine (or two) and your opponents don't have the ability to respond, they'll appear unorganized.

Do this in the right situations though—some local jams, will actually value taking single rounds to doing routines. Know the scene and respond accordingly. You must also give your opponents the ability to respond to one of your routines—if you choose to do a routine in your last round, you should go first so your opponent has the option to do a routine in response. Be careful about this, though—if your opponent does not have a routine to respond with, they will appear weak and unprepared. If they do a strong routine and blow you out, you'll look bad.

At a Jam – Get to know your local and regional scenes, and how they feel about routines. The sense that I have is that generally local jams tend to look down upon routines (because they are small and should be between individuals and personalities), while larger jams are meant to showcase the crew as a whole.

Of course, it is perfectly acceptable to do routines at a local jam for practice, but it might not go beyond the very fact of just practice. Typically, crew on crew battles, more commercial jams, and jams that emphasize crewnity are good places to use routines. Jams that are more "raw" or "real" would probably not value routines as much. Use your discretion and understand the scene and the culture of the jam itself.

When it is Not Appropriate to do Routines – It is inappropriate to do routines in a tie-breaker. Never do routines in a tie-breaker. Unless the MC or judges specifically say that you may use a routine, never use a routine in a tie-breaker; only go one on one. The reasons behind this are myriad, but they largely have to do with a tie-breaker being between representatives of the crew, and not the crew as a whole.

It is also not appropriate to do a routine as the last round of the battle when the opponent doesn't have the ability to respond. I often see crews do this, and it is a faulty way to approach routines. When doing a routine, you must give your opponent the chance to respond—not only will this allow the opponent the opportunity to do (possibly making them look good) or not do (making them look unorganized) a routine, but you will look stronger as a result. If you do a routine as a last round, you will not only look disorganized because you didn't have the ability to do the routine earlier, but it will look like you are scared—the crowd and judges will have perceived you as needing do a routine as a last ditch measure to win, and that you didn't want to give the other crew a chance to respond. If you choose to do a routine at the end of a battle, do so with caution and intention. Know your enemy.

ON CREW HYPE

Crew hype can be a very useful tool to commandeer the flow of a battle. Many crews prefer to stay as the strong, silent type when not on the dance floor—this is perfectly acceptable. Still, when you prefer not to be hype on the sidelines you should still be giving your crew positive energy with nods, silent props, high fives, and show that you're engaged in the battle.

When you do choose to use crew hype as a tool though, it can be extremely effective—giving verbal props to your crew, shouting encouragement, and staying actively engaged does several things: it can show the judges that you are hungry and want to battle, it will pump up your crew members on and off the floor, and it can intimidate your opponents. These things can often help you take the tide of the battle and sometimes win by sheer force of will.

I will note, however, that there can be a downside to crew hype— maintaining high levels of energy throughout a jam can be difficult, and if your crew hype starts to sag, you will appear as if you're unengaged and tired (because you've set a precedent for being hype earlier).

Additionally, being too hype can be perceived as a turnoff to the crowd and judges—if your level of hype is perceived as out of context for the moves that you're doing, you may get marked down for this. The very fact of your crew hype may seem out of context.

More importantly, if you and your crew become too hype, you'll be perceived as out of control. If one of your crewmembers does an amazing move and your crew wants to rush the floor to celebrate, this can be a good thing, and you can show dominance in doing so. Still, be careful about doing this too often or at inappropriate times, as you don't want to appear out of control.

ON BEING CALLED OUT IN A CREW BATTLE

Occasionally when you're in a crew versus crew situation, you or one of your crewmembers may get called out. Do not respond to the call out, but rather, send someone else. When you're being called out in a crew battle, the opponent is trying to manipulate your order of attack as a part of their strategy. Rather than letting them control your order of attack, go at your own pace as a method of throwing them off their flow.

ON NOT LEAVING YOURSELF OPEN IN BATTLES

Often times, I see bboys/bgirls leaving themselves open to burns and taunts without recognizing it. If you're stepping into a battle, you should know that to your opponent, you are fair game and they may try to do anything to embarrass you and gain the upper hand. It is not hard to deflect obvious burns and taunts, and there are a few simple rules you can do to minimize the risk of leaving yourself open:

Pay Attention – This is the most important of these rules. If you're paying attention, you'll probably see obvious burns coming and can simply put your hand up to deflect or just move away. If you're not paying attention in a battle, you'll probably get burned.

Don't Return Handshakes – Returning handshakes is not worth the risk. Even someone you think you're on good terms with may show the high five and reject you. If you get burned, you appear weak and out of control. If, however, you reject the high five by not reciprocating, people will see that you're serious and engaged in the battle. You have little to gain by returning a high five in a battle, and everything to show by rejecting it. Of course, when the battle is over, you must give the due props to your opponent—but when you're in a battle, you're battling.

Stand Up – Of the three rules, this is probably the one I see people breaking the most. You don't have to have a certain standing posture when you're battling, just be sure to stand up—this will show that you're ready and engaged in the battle. If your hands are on your knees, that means you're tired, and your opponent may make fun of your stamina. If you are sitting or squatting, your mobility is limited and you may take a cock to the face. Sitting and squatting is also a sign of defeat, and you will be perceived as having given up on the battle.

KEEPING YOUR ENERGY HIGH AT A JAM: HOW TO SURVIVE TO THE FINALS

Learning how to pace yourself at a jam is a very difficult skill. Especially your first few jams, or the first few times you find yourself winning battles, you may find yourself in a situation where you are so tired that you may be satisfied with losing simply because you don't want to have to keep battling. This is something that you can learn to overcome, and ultimately must overcome if you're going to win jams.

There are several elements to surviving to the finals that you must consider:

The Physical – Typically, jams run at least five hours, sometimes more. The very fact of being active for that long can be very draining, much less having to actually execute high level moves during that extended period of time. You must work to build your physical endurance while walking your Path so that your body does not betray you in a battle.

I'm an advocate of both practicing and cross training—if you can take two or three days a week to do "two a day" workouts, one of an extended cardio workout (running, biking, swimming, circuit training, basketball, soccer, &c.) and one of a full out bboy/bgirl practice, you'll probably run into about three hours of physical activity during that day. Getting this to be normal during your weekly routine will help build the endurance for jams.

Warming Up and Cooling Down – Another difficult aspect of jams is the fact that you'll be warming up and cooling down in preparation for the battle, after the prelims, and between rounds. This is something that you must be intentional about—when you've cooled down once, your body may start to go into recovery mode. Instead of trying to have this happen multiple times, stay at a place of "low warm," meaning that you're not full out and sweating, but you haven't completely cooled down. Continue to stretch, do light moves, and stay active. If you stay "low warm," you'll be able to maintain a similar level of activity throughout the jam—if you fully warm up and cool down, your physical rhythms will be thrown off and you can fatigue faster.

Sleep Before a Jam – The reality is that many bboys/bgirls practice at night, and we tend to embrace a culture of nocturnal artistry. Many bboys/bgirls go to bed late and get up late. I'm in no way advocating that you change your sleeping habits in terms of when you go to bed and when you wake up—what I am saying is that if you get a proper night's sleep of 7-9 hours before a jam, you will do better than if you sleep fewer hours. Be mature about it and get a

good night's sleep before the jam—if you want to go out, go out after the jam.

What You Eat and Drink Matters – Much in the same way that sleeping properly will help you before a jam, eating properly and hydrating will help you during a jam. You'll be more in tune with what works for your body, but generally avoid fried foods, foods that are high in unhealthy fats and oils, and foods high in sugar. Eat lots of healthy carbs, especially the night before and morning of a jam, as well as fruits, veggies, and protein. Drink water. If you take caffeine in your day to day, try not to switch things up the day of a jam—you might experience withdrawal.

Although it seems like common sense, do not drink too much alcohol before a jam if you want to do well. If you're hung over at the jam, it will negatively affect your performance—you'll lose some of your mental speed and dehydrate faster. Stay healthy.

Bring Changes of Clothes – If you're the type of bboy/bgirl that sweats a lot or you know the venue will be hot, bring several changes of clothes. Even if you aren't the type of bboy/bgirl that sweats, it is still important to have a change of clothes just in case. Not only will the sweat speed up your cooling-down process, you also risk getting sick if you're wearing wet clothes. Staying dry will help your endurance and health at a jam.

The Mental – Jams can be mentally draining. Not only are they long and eat up a great portion of your day, but you'll be around a lot of people you might not normally be with, you may be nervous about the battles, and the energy of the venue and participants will probably be running rampant (be it energy that is too high or too low). You must maintain control during this time—as I've talked about earlier, you have to keep your head above water and maintain your calm and focus. If you can maintain calm, you'll last throughout the jam. This is also something that you can develop through constant practice and study.

More Stick-to-it-iveness – By the end of a jam, everyone is usually tired. Your opponents have been through just as many rounds as you (unless you've done tie-breakers), and you may find it difficult to keep your energy high. In situations like this, you must force yourself to have high energy and manifest physicality to overcome your opponent. While not easy to do, you can practice for this—it helps to have a burst of physical energy at the end of a normal practice or workout. Make it a routine at practice to do something like going rounds, a cardio drill, or sprints. Learn to push yourself beyond the point that you're physically uncomfortable, and learn how to execute and show energy even when you're tired. If you can do this in your normal practice, you'll be comfortable pushing yourself at a jam.

Try Not to Watch Too Many Battles – While it is important to keep an eye on some of the battles at a jam to understand the brackets, who is in the tournament with you, and get a handle on how your opponents are doing that day, watching too many of the battles can be a detriment.

Not only will you stop your motion and risk cooling down by watching the battles, you may see something intimidating and be tempted to give in to the energy of the jam. Be smart about which battles you watch and maintain your focus. You're there to win, not to spectate.

BATTLE DRILLS

Much like I've provided in the Earth and Water Books, below are some practical drills to get yourself familiar with how to battle more effectively. Much of the above is a theoretical discussion that you may find difficult to put into practice—the below drills are meant to give you a means to practice some of the above concepts. Consider what you're working on when you do the following drills and be intentional about developing yourself and honing your tools.

LEARN TO BEAT ROUNDS
THAT ARE "EASY TO LOSE TO"

Especially when you're learning to battle and developing your own skills (and even after you've become relatively experienced), you might find yourself losing battles that you think you've won, or think you have the potential to win. Generally, you'll be losing these battles to bboys/bgirls that fit into the "Consistent Bboy/Bgirl" category as I've described above—while these bboys/bgirls might not blow you out of the water with big moves, they are consistent, solid, and generally difficult to beat.

To learn how to beat these rounds, you need to seek out a dancer that fits into this "Consistent Bboy/Bgirl" category, or a "Clutch" that can tone down their blow ups and power to help you practice. Have this bboy/bgirl do a set with the full package—toprock, some power, some floorwork, and end in a freeze. Have them execute the set calmly.

Then try to beat the round—take a moment to honestly evaluate how you did with the other dancer. It helps to video your rounds and watch them.

The trick to beating the "Easy to Lose to" sets is to do something slightly stronger or more unique than the other bboy/bgirl and execute your set fully. Beating these sets requires you to pay attention to details—direct your energy, use your weapons effectively, and execute. Consistent Bboys/Bgirls tend to do well at jams, but sometimes find it difficult to make it past semi-finals of their own accord. Often, they'll run up against someone with a stronger asset that stands out more than them—if you can demonstrate that you have these assets, you'll do well and beat the "Easy to Lose to" sets.

CREATING DESTRUCTIVE ROUNDS

Destructive rounds are very helpful to have in tight situations. When I say a "destructive" round, I mean a go down that has such power, blow ups, or unique movement that you can generally beat most sets. These are the type of rounds that are so strong at their base that your opponent could only do a more powerful "destructive" set to beat you, or you'll only lose if you don't execute the moves properly.

Figure out what moves build a strong tension or are strong enough in and of themselves that if you piece them together, you'll generally beat most opponents. The most difficult part of having a destructive set tends to be the execution—this is when "Utsu vs Ataru" comes into play. You must practice your destructive rounds until they become like second nature to you. Practice them in context battling with your crew or friends until you can pull them out consistently at any time. Focus on throwing these in context so that when put into a battle, you'll be able to do these moves effectively.

USING MUSICALITY

Whether or not you're the type of a bboy/bgirl that prefers to do power, tricks, or footwork, having musicality at your disposal is a very powerful tool. While it is important to dance on beat in your toprock, you should be able to interpret music at a higher level if you're going to be battling at higher level events.

Practice battling and going rounds to different songs at different tempos. First, get comfortable with dancing on beat. When you feel that you've mastered dancing on beat, begin to try to interpret different sounds in the song—not just the drum beat or horn that often comes on the "one" in the music, but pay attention to drum rolls, bass lines, horn sections, vocals, and different sounds that come out in the song. If you're intentional about learning to dance and do appropriate moves to these at practice, it will start to come out naturally in a battle.

Likewise, if you can do power or tricks on beat, or demonstrate that you have the full package in a battle, judges and the crowd will tend to view your dancing more favorably.

COUNTER BLOW UPS

Counter blow ups are extremely useful to have at your disposal, and one of the most effective ways to demonstrate control over your opponent. By "counter blow ups," I mean a move or a transition that you do immediately after your opponent finishes their set. Often you counter when they are still on the floor, and you simply do the move around or next to them. Generally, counter blow ups should only be one move, three or four at the most, including transitions. If you can calmly execute your counter blow up and intentionally move into your set (without losing control from too much hype), the counter blow up will give you huge marks in a battle.

One of the biggest mistakes that I see bboys/bgirls make is trying to elongate their counter blow ups—they'll do a power set that includes up to eight or ten rotations, or a complicated footwork pattern. They'll then get up and do toprock, then finish their set. Not only does this do away with the punch of having your move be a "counter," but it makes your round lop-sided, and severely hurts your round's pacing—in these cases, it would actually be more effective to simply make that power set or complicated footwork pattern the crux of your set, and just do it normally after toprock.

Determine several moves that are strong and preferably ones that travel, so you can dynamically enter the circle. From there, practice using these moves while going rounds or battling with friends and crewmembers. Generally, aggressive footwork, slides, flips, quick spins, and traveling power/tricks work well as counter blow ups. Again, I stress that a counter blow up is only one or two moves (three to four at most if you include transitions) that strike quickly.

LAYING TRAPS

Another tactic that is often misused by bboys/bgirls is laying a trap at the end of your set—many bboys/bgirls will lay a trap at the end of their round by creating the appearance that they have finished, and when their opponent comes out to start their set, they will hit the floor again so as to try to throw off the opponent. More often than not, the bboy/bgirl that lays the trap will do something without substance—a knee drop or simple footwork. This is done with the intention of demonstrating control over the opponent, but typically only serves the purpose of making the bboy/bgirl's set look disjointed and making the opponent look more controlled. Often, because bboys/bgirls are doing this at the end of their set, they are also tired and may mess up if they try to throw a hard move.

It is possible to lay a trap effectively, but understand that the risk is high. One of the most effective traps I've seen laid was by Napalm (Lions of Zion) when he battled Victor (MF Kids/Squadron) at the BC One North America qualifier in 2015. Watch the way he presents his traps, directs it, and executes quickly at the end of his first round.

You must do three things when laying a trap:

1. **Throw your opponent off balance.** This is easy to do as you simply have to have your opponent start to move. The problem is that if you don't do something with substance or execute,

your opponent can regain their balance. You must throw your opponent off balance and keep them from regaining it.

2. **Do something with substance and do it fast**. The formula of your trap is the same as a counter blow up. Only do one to three moves (or two to four with transitions) and have them hit hard. Don't waste time and don't do too much or your pacing will appear off.

3. **Execute**. Your entire set will be called into question if you don't execute your trap. Since you're doing this at the end of your set, it can become risky to do a hard move.

ENERGY FOCUS

Focusing your energy intentionally is a huge advantage when battling—not only does it tighten your set, but it tends to create cohesion throughout. Start by simply learning to make eye contact with your opponent when you battle—practice battle or go rounds with a friend or crewmember and try to make eye contact when doing your toprock. When you feel comfortable making eye contact when toprocking, learn to make eye contact when you're doing moves on the floor. While it may take some time to get comfortable doing so, you'll also want to try to make eye contact and direct your body to face your opponent when hitting freezes.

Once you're comfortable making eye contact and facing your opponent in battles, practice "losing" eye contact at different points during your set—do a spin, hit a powermove, or do a rotating footwork pattern—once you've lost eye contact, work to re-establish it. Try to learn how to "lose" and then "regain" focus on the opponent several times in a single round. It helps to learn how to do this intentionally in case you get lost in a battle—if you become lost, then you'll be able to refocus your energy and tie your set together.

Finally, learn how to control your energy at will—rather than mindlessly making eye contact with your opponent the entire round (which becomes one dimensional and boring), learn to turn away from the opponent intentionally, give them looks on beat, and direct certain moves to the opponent to create tension and drama. If you are directing your energy away from an opponent and then can focus all your energy on them in a single moment, you can intimidate them and control the pace of a battle. Additionally, the judges and crowd will see that you are both more focused and more in control if you can direct your energy with intention.

THE INTANGIBLE STUFF
ABOUT BATTLING

ON WINNING

You should always win gracefully. Showboating, excessive celebration, rubbing a victory in your opponent's face, and bragging are entirely unacceptable when you've won both a battle and a jam. I'm not suggesting that you don't enjoy your victory—after all, if you've won a jam, you most likely put a great deal of effort into doing so. Enjoy your victory, feel blessed in the moment, and celebrate in a way that doesn't make others feel bad. Keep in mind though, that in your moment of victory your opponents will be spurred by their defeat, and they'll be back to training. Don't dwell on your victory but rather, get back to training—a win is just one more step on the Path.

ON LOSING

As you should win gracefully, you should always lose gracefully. Whining, complaining, and talking trash are not acceptable after you've lost—keep in mind that if you lost, you didn't convince the judges beyond a reasonable doubt that you won the battle. Maintain grace especially in the moment of your loss, and get out of the battle cypher if you feel you can't maintain your composure. Cool off.

Once you've acknowledged your loss, objectively identify what happened. Figure out what you can do better, more of, less of, or differently to create a different outcome. Once you've identified and learned from what happened in the battle, get back to training. Be honest with yourself—it might be hard to revisit battles honestly, but it will help you identify what you can do better next time.

Do not, however, dwell on your loss. Once you know what you should learn from your loss, take the lesson but remove the sting from your mind. Don't watch a video of yourself crashing or messing up. Rather, work to better yourself and move on from the loss itself.

ON CALLING OUT THE JUDGES

I don't want to spent too much time with a discussion in this section, but it should be explicitly stated that it is acceptable to call out the judges. In fact, it is much more acceptable to call out the judges than complain, trash talk, or generally be upset after the battle. Hip Hop exists within a landscape where we must be willing to back ourselves up at all times, and judges must also be held accountable for the position that they are in.

With that said, if you decide to call out the judges, be aware that you may be perceived in a certain way, and call them out tactfully. The purpose of calling out the judges is to display to them, the crowd, and yourself that you have superior dancing skills. If you don't have the ability to back up your claim or smoke the judges, you'll appear silly.

ON KEEPING YOUR COOL IN BATTLE

While Hip Hop is a culture rooted in peace, unity, and love, with the fact of competition comes heightened emotions. When emotions run high and battles become intense, physical altercations may arise. The key to avoiding altercations in a battle is to train yourself physically, mentally, and emotionally at all times through my Heiho, such that you have no need to rely on violence to resolve disputes. Rather, you'll be able to understand and diffuse the situation before it rises to such a level.

With that said, it becomes difficult to maintain that level of cool all the time. The most effective technique for keeping cool in a battle is simply to check yourself. Don't react if your opponent accidentally hits you. Pay attention to the situation around you, and be ready if you see an opponent getting aggressive. Finally, remove yourself from the situation if you feel that you can't control yourself.

You may also find that your crewmates or friends will get heated in situations of battle. If that is the case, work to be preventative— when you see an altercation forming, pull them away. Take them out of the situation or pre-emptively diffuse something if it is starting to become toxic. Keep in mind that as dancers, we're supposed to resolve our disputes on the floor, not with fighting.

ON THE RHYTHMS OF THE INTERVALS

To know the rhythms of the intervals means to understand when an opponent has an opening. This can be useful for several reasons—

you don't need to trash talk exactly, but if you can show your opponent that you recognize a flaw in their dancing, simply giving them a cock of the head or an "I know you messed up" grimace can create unwanted tension in their set. Additionally, having an interval in their dancing means that you can capitalize on those moments—use their intervals to demonstrate your superiority. If the interval exists in footwork or power, demonstrate your superior footwork or power. Learn the rhythm of your opponent and take advantage of these moments.

"TO INJURE THE CORNERS"

By injuring the corners, you are attacking an opponent's "balance points" or weak points to weaken the opponent as a whole. You can do this several ways—if in a 1v1, your opponent may have deficiencies in their set that you can show your superiority to. If in a crew v. crew, you can actively attack one of the balance points by calling someone out, directing your energy at the weaker of the opponents, or by attacking and counter-attacking at certain points.

Consider a 4v4. If your opponent has dancers that are weaker, by defeating these weaker rounds, you can create the perception that the whole is weaker and win by this method. By attacking the balance points of an opponent, you can bring down a person or squad who may otherwise appear strong.

CONSIDERING THE SITE

While I've already discussed above how the venue and energy of the jam can affect you, it stands to reiterate that you must judge the details of the site and use them to your advantage. If there is a bright light in the venue, keep it behind you. If the ground is slanted (depending on the venue), take the higher ground. These small details can build an advantage for you, or do away with a potential disadvantage.

KNOW THE PREVAILING CONDITIONS

To know the prevailing conditions means to understand the situations surrounding your battle. Consider the conditions happening around you as if you were planning a trip. How you would prepare for it? Is it sunny? Is it raining? Is your car/boat/plane in good working condition? Will there be things getting in your way? The more prepared you can be by knowing the prevailing conditions, the more you will be able to set yourself up for success in a battle. While you should be in tune with the conditions of your own physical and mental states, below are several things to consider when entering a battle:

Knowing the Spirit of the Opponent – Pay attention to the morale of your opponent. Are they entering the battle hungry, do they have a neutral attitude, or are they tired and feeling defeated? You should always prepare for the worst, but also understand that the state of your opponent can help shape your plan of attack. If you know that they'll be attacking strong, prepare yourself for strong counterattacks and use their momentum against them. If their morale is neutral, you can hijack the pace of the battle. If your opponent's morale is low, you can use your force to demoralize them further and win without question.

Find Their Strengths and Weaknesses – I've discussed a great deal above in both the Water and Fire books about how to play to your strengths and demonstrate your opponent's weaknesses, but you should pay attention to their conditions on that particular day. Don't allow yourself to showcase your opponent's strengths by leaving yourself open, and be in tune with their weaknesses.

Plot Against their Expectations – Whether or not they are intentional about doing so, your opponents will also be coming to the battle with a set of expectations—while they might not be able to articulate that they've evaluated the prevailing conditions, they'll intuitively have a sense of what the battle with you will be like. Consider how you are being perceived, and plot against their expectations. If this means going out first, do so. If this means changing the order of attack in your squad, do so. If this means doing a different set, do so. Weigh how much the element of surprise will work against your opponent and strike against their expectations.

Know Their Rhythms – As mentioned above, there is a rhythm to all things (not just the rhythm of music, but the rhythm of winning, losing, dancing well, dancing poorly, &c.). Get to know your opponent's rhythms as well. Do they perform better under certain conditions? Do they like some songs or situations better than others? Is their rhythm off when they have to respond to a certain attack? By knowing your enemy and their rhythms, you can strike at their corners.

TO KNOW COLLAPSE

> "[T]here are usually times during the conflict when the rhythm of the opponent goes haywire and he begins to collapse...
> It is important to keep an eye out for such a collapse and to strike with certainty so that the opponent does not have the opportunity to recover." – Musashi

This should be relatively straightforward in terms of battles. You will find yourself in situations when your opponent (be it in 1v1s or crew battles) will self-destruct. You'll also find that sometimes because there is a lack of tension caused by this mess up, that you or your crew may respond by messing up. Know that when your enemy does collapse, you must capitalize on this opportunity not by responding with a weak or even mediocre set, but by completely destroying the opponent and commandeering the flow of the battle. Especially if you're facing a strong opponent that may be able to recover from a collapse, you have to hit hard at this opportunity so that they cannot recover.

TO BECOME THE ENEMY

> "In Heiho as it pertains to large numbers, one [tends to] think(s) of the opponents as strong and becomes passive." – Musashi

To become the enemy simply means to put yourself in your enemy's shoes—this is similar to considering the prevailing conditions, but should also be taken as a way to increase your confidence in yourself. You'll tend to perceive your opponent as stronger than they are—while you should take your opponent seriously and attack them without hesitation, know that your opponent is also coming to the battle with a set of expectations and sometimes, apprehensions.

They'll also be perceiving you as a strong threat. Know that this is the case and have confidence in how you're being perceived.

> "In large-scale battles, when the enemy starts to employ a particular tactic, if you show him your determination to check him, your enthusiasm will overwhelm him and he will change his tactics." - Musashi

As mentioned above, both you and your opponent will be coming to the table with different expectations. If you can successfully strike back and defend against their strong tactics, your sheer will of force will help you overcome them. Even if you are scared, don't show that you're intimidated in battle. Use your attacks to rebuff the opponent.

ON REPEATING IN BATTLES

If you find yourself winning in earlier rounds of jams and making it to top eight, semi-finals, and finals, you may begin to face the problem of repeating moves in battle. If you find yourself repeating moves, you'll simply need to go back to the lab and create more vocabulary. If you have the vocabulary but you're still repeating, you need to learn to incorporate it more organically.

Judges tend to have different philosophies on how bad it is to repeat in battles—some look down upon it to the point that they'd have you lose the battle simply because you're repeating. Others will still give you points for the move you've repeated, just not as many.

However the judges themselves perceive what you're doing, know that it is unacceptable to repeat too much in a battle, and that you must find ways to be more versatile and unpredictable. If you continue to repeat the same moves, the crowd and judges will get bored, and you'll find it difficult to continue advancing in battles— eventually, you'll also start to hit a wall at larger jams when you show your lack of versatility.

There are several other layers to the issue of repeating and lack of versatility. Especially in the United States and at 1v1 battles abroad, well rounded bboys/bgirls tend to do better—this is because within the States and in 1v1s, the culture of the competition values well-roundedness. However, in a crew on crew, it becomes less obvious if you repeat, and you'll probably do fewer rounds. If you have only one or two rounds of killer power that you can pull out and blow shit up, that can actually be acceptable. Know, however, that if you only have those two rounds, you probably won't do as well in 1v1 or 2v2 situations because it will be obvious that you're repeating.

The other layer has to do with creating variations on transitions of the moves. The two bboys that come to mind for this are Ryoma from Mortal Combat and Luan from Funk Fockers. Both these bboys are good examples of dancers that have done well on the world stage, but really only have one extremely powerful move: the airchair. Both of these bboys have interesting style, some power and footwork (Luan tends to have strong footwork in general), but the strength of both these bboys comes from the incredible variation they have in their airchair transitions. They've both developed combos, tricks, powermoves, and unique blowups all stemming from the airchair. If you have a single move that you feel drawn to and want to rely upon, know that like Ryoma and Luan, it is possible to work around and be creative with that move to make yourself competitive.

ON CYPHER BATTLES

My primary concern in the Book of Fire is the judged bboy/bgirl battle, but because cypher battles are such an important part of your life as a dancer, you should also be prepared for them. Know that cypher battles are different than judged battles—it doesn't always matter who does technically better in a cypher battle, but how you and your opponent are being perceived. In this way, cypher battles tend to be much closer to a natural encounter between two parties, and is more of a clash of energy. Consider some of the following:

Number of Moves – When you're cypher battling, it is just as important not to repeat moves and concepts as if you were battling in a judged bboy/bgirl battle. You will appear limited in your arsenal if you repeat moves—even if you have to use retired moves or shorten your sets, it can be better than repeating concepts. Remember that cypher battles highly value posture and appearance, and you want to maintain a strong image in a cypher battle, even if you have to fake this.

Length of Rounds – Cypher battles tend to be a much faster, abbreviated conversation when compared to judged battles. While judged battles are like a formal debate in which each party is given an allotted time and is then expected to adhere to the rules, a cypher battle is more akin to a natural conversation (or even argument). In this way, shorter rounds that make a quick point tend to do well for the medium. Likewise, because cypher battles often become a test of endurance and will, you'll want to keep your rounds to a manageable length.

Endurance – Outlasting your opponent is one of the most important aspects of the cypher battle. Again, so much of cypher battling has to do with the appearance that you create through the battle and the posture that you have. If you can show that you can dance longer than your opponent, not get tired, and you still want to keep dancing, you'll have a stronger chance of appearing to win. Of course, your rounds up to that point should have had solid content, but you must strike the balance of maintaining endurance and quality in your sets.

The Meta-Battle – Cypher battles usually happen for a reason. Sometimes they are simply a matter of being in the "right place at the right time," (or the wrong place, depending on how you look at it), but more often than not they occur because a bboy/bgirl wants to test themselves, they respect a bboy/bgirl and want to battle, or because two bboys/bgirls or crews have beef that they want to try to resolve.

When considering how you approach the cypher battle, also consider that what happens there will be part of a longer narrative and relationship between yourself and the other party. If an up and coming bboy/bgirl is challenging you, they'll probably come at you hard and want to use you as a stepping stone to prove that they are getting better—and you could do the same. Know that if the battle is a beef battle, you should try to prove your point but try not to make the relationship between the two parties worse as a result—you're conversing through the dance and trying to settle a dispute between two parties.

When engaging in a cypher battle, understand that the battle is a result of converging forces up until that point, and that the battle itself is a medium with which to move those forces.

The Crowd – Crowds in cypher battles tend to be a makeup of the crewmembers of those involved. The crowd will be weighted heavier towards one party or the other with fewer third party onlookers than a normal crowd may have. As a result, the crowd will usually be in tune with the significance of what is happening during the battle. Sometimes, crewmembers will even get involved. Much in the same way that you should consider the meta-battle, the crewmembers here can become more significant and more interactive in cypher battles than judged bboy/bgirl battles.

ON JAMS

Since jams are where judged battles take place, I want to discuss jams and some tools for how you can approach them. Keep in mind that you must balance the "business" aspect of battling at a jam with the fact that jams are supposed to be fun and you should enjoy being with your crew and friends and dancing to music. Jams will far too often feel like an intense competition. While sometimes you should approach them with intensity, you should also cultivate the ability to enjoy yourself at jams.

GOING TO JAMS

Initially, it can be hard to break into going to jams. The internet has made jams easier to find, but only if you know where to look. Talk with friends and people at your practice space about possible upcoming jams and get a feel for the scope. If you've not battled before, you may want to go to a few local jams (or even some large ones) to get a sense of how jams work. Seeing so much energy in one place may be intimidating at first, but you'll be able to get a handle on your own energy if you follow the techniques that I've outlined above.

If you're new to battling, start small and be patient with yourself. Try to enter local jams and don't immediately try to enter anything that is too high level. Before you get into situations that are too intense, you'll want to build up to them—set yourself up for success by starting locally and branch out from there.

When you start to build a rep and think about "blowing up," you'll probably start wanting to go to jams for a reason. It can still be important to go to small jams in the local community to help build up other bboys/bgirls and show face, but if you're competing, it should be to better yourself. Reject the idea that you could ever lose anything by battling—everyone loses battles and everyone gets upset in some situations. Each battle is another step on the Path and you should grow from it. With that said, though, you should gauge whether going to some jams are worth it for you.

PRACTICING AT LOCAL JAMS

Local jams are a great place not only to start building your reputation in your town and get to know other dancers, but after you've reached a certain level, they can be taken as practice. Especially at small jams, you can try out new material in a low pressure environment. By becoming comfortable doing moves at a local jam, you'll get used to putting together rounds in a "battle" environment—in this way, small jams are low stress, but the type of environment where you'll get used to executing.

While you don't want to battle at so many local jams that it becomes frustrating for the community (if you win them), it can help by being a presence to raise the scene. Additionally, you can benefit from battling since it will allow you to stay in the zone—many find it easy to slide out of the "battle mode" and get rusty, so by trying to stay consistent through battling locally, it will better prepare you for larger events.

GOING TO RELEVANT JAMS

While battling at local jams can be great practice and community builders, you won't be able to raise your rep, learn new styles, and clash with stronger bboys/bgirls (and become stronger in the process) unless you start going to relevant jams. If you live in a large city with a strong scene, you may be lucky enough to have relevant jams close to you. If you live in the suburbs or a rural area though, you may have to travel to go to relevant jams.

Since jams are simply an entity comprised of all the people attending, pay attention to the people to determine whether or not the jam is relevant. Are strong crews going? Are there any bboys/bgirls that you look up to and could learn from? Are there any bboys/bgirls that you want to battle? How many competitors will be from out of town? Also, pay attention to the DJ and the host— if they throw and perform at quality jams, it would probably be a benefit for you to go.

IT'S OKAY NOT TO GO TO JAMS

Much of what I've talked about in the Water and Fire books has to do with balance between two opposing forces. Much in the same way, you must balance whether or not you should go to some jams. Keep in mind your reason for going to jams. I'm hesitant to say "what you can gain," from going to a jam, but this isn't a bad way to look at it—there should be a purpose in going to a jam, even if you don't "benefit" per se. What I mean is this—it's ok to go to a jam to hang out with friends, because you want to support the host,

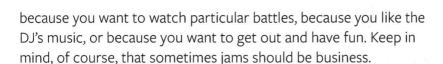

because you want to watch particular battles, because you like the DJ's music, or because you want to get out and have fun. Keep in mind, of course, that sometimes jams should be business.

With all this said, it is also ok not to go to jams—just because there is a jam in town doesn't necessarily mean you have to go. If you won't benefit from battling, if you need some time to rest (resting is part of training), if you have family or business affairs to attend to, or if something comes up, you shouldn't stress about not going to a jam. Keep the aspect of balance in mind—go to jams with purpose and keep your tools sharp, but don't go so hard as to break yourself.

AVOIDING IRRELEVANT JAMS

This section could be an extension of the "it's okay not to go to jams" section, but with a slight difference. The above implies that these are jams that you might want to go to, but don't necessarily need to or won't benefit from going to. Be aware that there are irrelevant jams that you should actively avoid. These jams may include jams hosted by people that don't have ties to the Hip Hop world (and are trying to exploit the fact of having a "dance battle"), jams hosted by unorganized or unknowing parties, or jams that aren't geared towards dancers (i.e. you are not the target audience for attendance).

Since you will have nothing to gain from attending irrelevant jams, and conversely, they could become a damage to your psyche and you may risk injury as a result, you should avoid irrelevant jams at all costs. Irrelevant jams, however, are different than "wack" jams, which I'll also talk about below. Consider that irrelevant jams are simply those that are inconsequential and where you stand nothing to gain from.

AVOIDING WACK JAMS

Irrelevant jams are the types of jams that don't matter and you stand to gain nothing from them. Wack jams, however, are an active detriment to the scene and work to destroy our culture.

These can be difficult to spot, though, and you'll probably feel the pull to go to these jams because they'll appear to be relevant—often for different reasons. The reality is that you'll probably attend a few wack jams over the course of your career—that's okay though. You should learn to spot wack jams, and with the tools below, you'll be able to get some context in recognizing when you've attended a wack jam and figure out how to avoid them in the future.

WHAT MAKES A WACK JAM WACK?

As mentioned above, wack jams are an active detriment to the Hip Hop scene. They don't contribute to bboy/bgirl culture, but work to exploit our art and take our money (however minimal it may be) and don't give us anything in return. These jams can be large and commercial, or small and local. Whatever the case, these jams typically showcase bboys/bgirls without demonstrating the art form in its proper element—wack jams are often populated by a high number of non-dancers without the context to understand what we're doing or what moves are dope. While irrelevant jams may leave you feeling nothing (and sometimes frustrated because you've gained nothing), wack jams may leave you with a sense of loss.

HOW TO SPOT WACK JAMS

There are myriad ways to spot a wack jam. You'll get a better sense of what they are, but here are some telltale signs:

- Jams that use the word "breakdance."
- Jams that are crowd judged.
- Jams that are part of a larger festival and details aren't given about the battles (i.e. the event is from noon to midnight, and there will be a battle at some point).
- Jams that don't have an odd number of judges.
- Jams where the host isn't a bboy/bgirl or Hip Hop aficionado that is an active part of the scene.
- Jams that don't have the details specified (who is judging, the DJ, the format).
- Jams that haven't run on time in the past (or close to it—even Hip Hop time of +/- two hours).
- Jams where the bboy/bgirl battle (or dancing in general) isn't the main event.

Among these more obvious signs of a wack jam, there are other indicators where you can use your own judgement to determine whether or not the jam might possibly be wack:

Jams That Try to do Too Much – A possible indicator of a wack jam is a jam that tries to do too much. Take for instance a jam that has an MC battle, a graff battle, a bboy/bgirl battle, all styles battles, four shows, and several exhibitions. While I like the idea that these things can co-exist at the same event, usually they don't work in practice simply because there is too much going on—often in too small a space. As much planning as the promoters try to do prior to the event, if they are juggling a full plate, the reality is that something will get pushed aside, and often times it will be the bboy/bgirl battle.

Jams That Don't Give Back to the Community – This is a bit more subjective and can be difficult to gauge, especially before going to the event. Generally though, jams that give back to the community will highlight your talent as bboys/bgirls, give you a place to battle, and will reward you for your effort. They put the bboys/bgirls first, want people to do well in battles, like hype at the event, and don't care so much if famous bboys/bgirls show up. Again, this can be difficult to gauge, but you can use your judgement—look at the promoter, the venue, and generally the way the jam is set up—if it feels like the jam is there to help the bboys/bgirls get better and sharpen their craft, it is probably a good sign. If you feel like the bboys/bgirls have to pay too much money, aren't getting anything in return, or are a novelty and there are too many non-dancers in the audience, this is a bad sign.

Jams Where You're a Part of the Show – You'll sometimes come across jams (usually part of a bigger festival or dance competition) where bboys/bgirls are "part of the show." This is the "bboys/bgirls as novelty" concept that I indicated above, and generally this is a telltale sign of a wack jam. If the bboy/bgirl battle is something that is at an event because the promotor wants the event to be more "street" or "raw," but doesn't really understand Hip Hop culture, that's probably a bad sign. If the crowd tends to give more love to the bboys/bgirls with the straightforward and easy to understand style (which, mind you, isn't a bad thing in some circumstances), and don't understand the bboys/bgirls who are executing more complex concepts, you're probably dancing for the wrong crowd. It can sometimes feel good to get easy props, but this will not help you as a dancer, and will become a detriment to your progress. The path to easy props is short and wide—the Path to true artistry is long and difficult.

Showcase Jams with no Return – Much like the above jams where you're a part of the show, there are some jams where you may or may not be a showcase, but you get nothing in return. While I don't think that prize money is always the best indicator of a good jam (sometimes wack jams give out good prize money, sometimes dope jams don't give much out), if you win you should be compensated fairly. I must emphasize that when I say "fairly," I mean to say that the promoter must meet the expectation that they've set out with from the start. If you're battling at a benefit jam where all proceeds are going to a cause, you shouldn't expect to win money.

However, if the jam promises to give out $100.00 for the win, you should expect to receive $100.00 for the win. Jams that do not deliver on these things are not worth your time and should be crushed from the community.

Jams That Have Lots of Invited Crews – Jams that have lots of invited crews can be toxic, because they don't create a level playing field. If a jam is going to go to the top 16 crews, and the host has invited 10 crews, the prelim field is battling for one of six spots. Not only is this unfair to those hoping for a spot, but it says something about the culture of the jam—the promoter is less concerned about fairness and equality than they are about having famous bboys/bgirls and big name crews involved. Although these jams can sometimes be relevant because of the bboys/bgirls involved, I dislike the attitude that leads to these jams.

I do have the make the distinction, however, between "invited" crews and "qualified" crews. At competitions like Freestyle Session or R-16, it is declared from the outset that there will be crews that have won regional qualifiers and automatically get a seat in top 16. Since the crew in theory has already "battled" their way to this status, and because the promoter has made it clear that there will be qualified crews occupying a space in the competition, this is acceptable in my opinion.

The jams that invite crews simply because of the merit perceived by the host, however, should be avoided if you can help it.

Get to Know the Host – Understanding the host of the jam (the promoter) is probably the single easiest way to understand whether or not a jam will be good. If the promoter has a history of throwing good events, you can assume that the upcoming event will probably be a good one. If the promoter is a bboy/bgirl who hasn't hosted very many events but is trying to get their feet wet and throw an event, it will probably be worth going to.

If the promoter is a company or someone you've never heard of, be wary—especially of companies throwing an event. They'll create expectations that they might not be able to fulfill. Likewise, be wary of someone that you've never heard of who throws an event. While they may be able to host a decent event, there is a strong possibility they don't know what a jam looks like, and they'll be using their preconceptions of what a jam should be (possibly informed by movies and commercial culture) to form the event. The results are often less than ideal.

Don't Go if the Judges are Wack – I don't necessarily mean to say that you shouldn't go if you consider the judges to be wack bboys/bgirls. Often times there are bboys/bgirls in the scene that have a strong understanding of the dance, but might not be the best dancers themselves—under certain circumstances, it is acceptable to have these bboys/bgirls as judges. By "wack" judges, I mean to say the jam's judges are the crowd, the judges are randomly selected from the audience, or the judges are simply not in the dance scene. Sometimes, even good bboys may not qualify as a judge because they have a low bboy/bgirl IQ. Keep it a matter of trust—if the judge is a mediocre bboy/bgirl but you generally trust their judgement, they could make a solid judge. If the judge is a random person or someone with an antiquated notion of what bboys/bgirls should be, avoid the jam. Also avoid jams that don't specify the judges prior to going.

Don't go if the DJ is Wack – Again, this could be another matter of opinion. Sometimes DJs have off days, and you might like a particular DJ some days and not others. Generally speaking though, you'll have a strong sense of a DJ's repertoire and vocabulary for songs. If you don't like their library, just don't go. Unless there is a very powerful draw for you in the event, you probably don't want to be dancing to wack music all night.

Know If You Should Go On Time – Going to jams on time or not can be a huge drain on your energy. As a general rule of thumb, jams run on bboy/bgirl time, so being late will be on time—I hate to admit that this is true, but if you show up as soon as the jam starts you'll be the only one there. Here are a few indicators to figure out how late you can show up to a jam:

The Venue – Is the venue contracted at a rec center, studio or gym (i.e. the promoter is paying by the hour to have the venue)? If yes, you'll probably get out on time because the promoter won't want to spend more money (or is getting kicked out). Is the venue an open space (park, place that the promoter has connections to, 24-hour establishment, bar, art gallery that is always open)? If yes, you can assume that the jam will run late.

The Size/Format – You should have a gauge of how big the event will be (100 people and 20ish crews, 300 people and 50ish crews... that sort of thing). The bigger the jam, the more time the promoter will need, and the more urgency to start early. If it's a 1v1 and the promoter has lots of time, it probably won't run on time.

The Start Time – Is the jam noon to midnight with battles that start at 2pm? It will run late. Is the jam 5pm to 10pm? It will be as close to on time as a bboy/bgirl jam can be. The more time the promoter allows for the jam, the more room they'll have to keep you waiting.

Here are a few examples: A local 2v2 at your town's YMCA that runs from 5pm to 10pm. Chances are that the event will run close to on time—battles will have to start at 6:30pm or 7pm to get you out by 10pm. The YMCA will want you out on time.

A local 1v1 at a bar that runs from 5pm to midnight. The bar probably won't close until 2am and the promoter won't have much of a sense of urgency to get you out on time. You could be there all night, and battles might not start until 10pm.

A high level crew v. crew with lots of out of towners that runs from 2pm to 10pm at a local gym. This might be a bit more difficult to gauge, but battles will probably start close to on timish (4pm or 5pm) simply because of the size of the event.

Consider the variables and use your judgement. You'll be able to figure out an appropriate time to give yourself and prepare for the battles.

ADVICE TO INTERNATIONAL PASSENGERS ON CARRIER LIABILITY

Passengers on a journey involving an ultimate destination or a stop in a country other than the country of departure are advised that international treaties known as the Montreal Convention, or its predecessor, the Warsaw Convention, including its amendments, may apply to the entire journey, including any portion thereof within a country. For such passengers, the treaty, including special contracts of carriage embodied in applicable tariffs, governs and may limit the liability of the carrier in respect of death of or injury to passengers, and for the destruction or loss of, or damage to, baggage, and for the delay of passengers and baggage. For additional information on international baggage liability limitations, including domestic portions of international journeys, see AA.com.

NOTICE OF INCORPORATED TERMS OF CONTRACT

Air Transportation, whether it is domestic or international (including domestic portions of international journeys), is subject to the individual terms of the transporting air carriers, which are herein incorporated by reference and made part of the contract of carriage. Other carriers on which you may be ticketed may have different conditions of carriage. International air transportation, including the carrier's liability, may also be governed by applicable tariffs on file with the U.S. and other governments and by the Warsaw Convention, as amended, or by the Montreal Convention. Incorporated terms may include, but are not restricted to: 1. Rules and limits on liability for personal injury or death, 2. Rules and limits on liability for baggage, including fragile or perishable goods, and availability of excess valuation charges, 3. Claim restrictions, including time periods in which passengers must file a claim or bring an action against the air carrier, 4. Rights of the air carrier to change terms of the contract, 5. Rules on reconfirmation of reservations, check-in times and refusal to carry, 6. Rights of the air carrier and limits on liability for delay or failure to perform service, including schedule changes, substitution of alternate air carriers or aircraft and rerouting.

You can obtain additional information on items 1 through 6 above at any U.S. location where the transporting air carrier's tickets are sold. You have the right to inspect the full text of each transporting air carrier's terms at its airport and city ticket offices. You also have the right, upon request, to receive (free of charge) the full text of the applicable terms incorporated by reference from each of the transporting air carriers. Information on ordering the full text of each air carrier's terms is available at any U.S. location where the air carrier's tickets are sold. Additionally, American Airlines' contract terms are found on AA.com under the "Legal" link. You can reach American Airlines on the web, using the following link: www.aa.com/customerrelations.

REV. 3/11

THE BOOK OF WIND

THE BOOK OF WIND

The Wind Book is concerned primarily with other schools of thought and attitudes towards bboying/bgirling. While the Earth Book lays the foundation for your understanding of my Heiho, the Water Book outlines the central tenants, and the Fire Book discusses the concept of battle, the Wind Book is meant to touch on some of the other ideas that exist in the bboy/bgirl ethos. This is not meant to be comprehensive, and it is not meant to draw negative attention to any bboys/bgirls specifically. Rather, the Wind Book is meant to be a discussion of why some attitudes and ideas in bboying/bgirling are negative, and my hope is to equip you with the tools to make informed decisions as you walk your Path.

Additionally, the discussion that follows is meant to help you gain the tools you need to evaluate the opinions and dance philosophies of others as you encounter them. It is faulty to think that you could become a successful dancer without exploring ideas beyond your own—not only should you work with allies, but I must again emphasize that you must know your enemy. Only by understanding your enemy (and other schools of thought), can you truly know and articulate your own Way. My hope is that you will keep an open mind when reading this book and use your imagination to figure out how this can apply to other aspects of your dancing and your life in general.

ABOUT PEOPLE WHO SPECIALIZE

There are some bboys/bgirls (especially internationally) who specialize in one aspect of the dance. While this can serve to help them become famous, the fame tends to be both short-lived and without much substance—the bboys/bgirls that get known for only one aspect of their dance usually have very little overall substance to what they are doing.

While it is important to have a specialty in the modern world (and specialization helps in the professional environment), it is important to develop your skills as a well-rounded dancer and person. In battles as well as life, you'll be put into a variety of situations—if your skill set is specialized, that is fine, but you'll need a variety of skills to thrive in a variety of situations. Different battles call for different things, and if you are inflexible or haven't developed your skills, your reliance upon that single asset will become apparent.

Again, I'm not telling you that specialization is a bad thing—bboys/bgirls that specialized in powermoves or footwork have helped push the bounds of those aspects of the dance. What I dislike is the mindset that would create too much reliance upon a single thing. You must be willing to step outside of yourself and develop a variety of skills, and become a well-rounded individual so that you can be successful in any environment. You must work at this constantly.

ON BBOYS/BGIRLS THAT RELY TOO MUCH ON THEIR MOVES, TECHNIQUE, OR DANCING

I do believe that you should constantly be refining your technique and conditioning your body—only through constant practice and discipline can you become a strong dancer and continue to improve your skills. I also agree that you shouldn't rely too much upon something like trash-talking in battles, and that your skills should be able to speak for themselves. I do, however, also believe that reliance only upon your technique and the moves themselves can be a negative thing.

You should develop yourself such that you understand how to pace a battle, how to use your energy, and how to manipulate your opponent so that you can win a battle. The mindset that relies too much on technique and moves does not recognize that there are

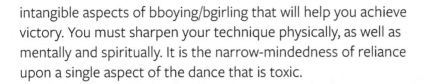

intangible aspects of bboying/bgirling that will help you achieve victory. You must sharpen your technique physically, as well as mentally and spiritually. It is the narrow-mindedness of reliance upon a single aspect of the dance that is toxic.

ON BBOYS/BGIRLS
THAT STAY ON THE DEFENSIVE

When I talk about bboys/bgirls that stay on the defensive I mean to say those that don't enter a battle with the spirit to win. It is acceptable to defend at certain points in the battle when you have the ultimate intention of claiming victory, but those that stay on the defensive are those that have no intention of winning. Often bboys/bgirls will enter jams just for the sake of entering jams—sometimes they will cite that they are entering for fun or for "experience." I can subscribe to the thought that you'd want to enter a jam for fun (after all, Hip Hop should be enjoyable), but typically these bboys/bgirls get put in a situation where they realize they'd want to win a battle—because of the tension created by the lack of seriousness and preparation, they sometimes sabotage themselves and their efforts and the "fun" factor turns negative. Likewise, the bboys/bgirls that enter for "experience" should enter every battle hoping to win. If you like the experience of being in a tight situation or close battle to help yourself get better, you're hindering your progress by entering with the thought of losing on your mind. In this way, the defensive stance can become counterproductive to your efforts. Whatever reason brings you into a battle, you should stick to that reason, and keep the reality of your efforts in mind.

MORE ON STAYING ON THE DEFENSIVE - RELYING ON YOUR "STANCE"

"Relying on your stance" means that you rely too much on your predetermined attitudes and maintain rigidity in your dancing and attitude as you enter a battle. If you enter a battle with too much rigidity and are unwilling to move from your stance (pre-existing dispositions) and take steps towards victory, your stance will become defensive and you'll lose your ability to go for the win. Another way to put this is that you have sets that you're absolutely going to do without thought of the music or what the enemy does—if you see that you could benefit from dancing to a certain song or countering a certain move that your enemy does, you should do this. The rigidity that makes bboys/bgirls stick to their stance is one that can lead toward failure.

> "One must irritate the stance of the other side, by designing strategies which the opponent would never foresee, by confusing, upsetting, or frightening the opponent, or by agitating him so as to break his rhythm. Thus it is said in the path of my Niten Ichiryu school that 'there is and there is not a stance.'" - Musashi

The idea here is that your "stance" is something that you do when there is no opponent around. In other words, your stance is your plan before the battle or the moves that you've practiced. When you are facing your opponent though, you don't rely on this "stance" as a defensive posture if you need to use these moves or ideas, it should be a pass through (the idea that a "move is not a move" as discussed in the Water Book). In the same way, you can pass through postures and stances in a battle to beat your opponent.

ON YOUR POINT OF CONCENTRATION IN BATTLES

There are some bboys that argue that your point of concentration should always be on your opponent in battles. This is taking the idea of a battle and an exchange far too literally. By point of concentration I do not mean to say where you are directing your energy. Point of concentration means what (or where) you are focusing on during the battle. If you focus too much on any one thing, you may miss other aspects of the battle—again consider the idea that if you pay attention to the forest, you fail to see the individual trees, but if you pay attention to the trees, you fail to see the forest.

Musashi explains that "if one attempts to fix one's point of concentration on one thing, the result will be wavering of the spirit and a hampering of Heiho." He goes on to give the analogy of a juggler—the juggler does not have to concentrate on the objects to see them—he is accustomed to seeing them without concentrating on them. Musashi tells us that, "[i]n Heiho, one may generally consider the spirit of the other person to be the subject of the point of concentration."

When putting this in terms of a bboy/bgirl battle, you should be accustomed to the music and the moves that you're doing already from diligent practice. In the same way, you shouldn't be focused on the individual moves that the opponent is doing too much (it's good to judge how much you should do, but don't let it in—you may become intimidated or distracted—rather, "see" the moves objectively). Rather, when battling, we should see the big picture and understand the spirit of the enemy. Focus on that and act from there. If you focus too much on the details, you'll lose your own flow and throw off your Heiho. If you focus too much on the big picture, you'll fail to see what's happening around you. Consider all this thoroughly.

ON SPEED IN BBOYING/BGIRLING

Many bboys/bgirls assert that the faster you do moves, the better—even these bboys/bgirls understand that there are tempo changes, but the very fact of speed must be treated differently than just a matter of doing the moves. Musashi tells us that "Speed is the fastness or the slowness which occurs when the rhythm is out of synchronization...if the opponent is hastening, it is important to resist this tendency and to remain calm so as to avoid being manipulated by the other side."

If you have ever felt that you were moving too fast or too slow—not just in bboying but in general—this is what Musashi is talking about. When in dancing, you may have tried to toprock or do footwork too quickly (or slowly), only to realize that you are not in rhythm. Likewise, in your day to day life you may have encountered instances where you were short on time and rushing through tasks, or days when you felt slower than normal—these are all examples of the "speed" that Musashi is discussing here.

The emphasis in a discussion of "speed" is to go at your own pace and do things at your own rhythm. As I discussed in the Water Book, everything has its own rhythm—doing well, doing poorly, winning, losing. When you are out of these rhythms, you'll experience fastness or slowness. As a dancer and in battles, your job is to stay calm, and maintain your natural rhythm.

Especially when you are at jams or in a battle, your opponent or those around you may be nervous or hype, and they'll move quickly (sometimes even out of their own rhythm). Your job is to ignore their rhythm and go at your own. This can become difficult when you're nervous or there is a lot of nervous energy at a jam—you may notice that people are dancing harder than normal. When you find yourself in these situations, step back and find your rhythm—it

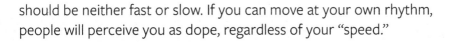

should be neither fast or slow. If you can move at your own rhythm, people will perceive you as dope, regardless of your "speed."

ON BBOYS/BGIRLS
WHO ARE NARROW-MINDED

I touched on this in the discussion of bboys/bgirls who specialize, but it is worth its own section. Like I said above, I dislike the spirit that would lead to a reliance on a particular weapon in bboying/ bgirling. Much in the same way, I dislike the spirit that would lead bboys/bgirls to be overly biased or overly favor a particular way of thinking. Again, this has more to do with the spirit behind the action. I understand that as bboying/bgirling is a subjective art, there is inherently a certain amount of bias that comes to the table. We as dancers and artists, though, should come to the table willing to see and evaluate new styles and new opinions with fresh eyes.

Bboying/bgirling reached the level it is at today because people were willing to be open-minded and try new things. Look around yourself for inspiration. Consider the opinions of other non-dancer artists and technicians. Be open to feedback. Even if you don't agree with it, it is important not just to reject these things, but understand why you don't agree with the feedback they've given you. If you can understand this and intentionally move on, this is acceptable. Also give weight to the opinions of others and evaluate from a point of neutrality. If you aren't paying attention to what is happening around you, you'll stunt your own growth.

THE BOOK OF EMPTINESS

THE BOOK OF EMPTINESS

PREFACE

The shortest of the books in Musashi's *Book of Five Rings,* the Book of Emptiness (or Void) is a meditation on humans, our relationship to the universe, and the very nature of knowledge itself. The Book of the Void leaves a number of things to interpretation, with elements of spirituality, philosophy, and some pieces that may be even argued as Platonic (in the original sense of the word) from a Western perspective.

Musashi draws upon the Buddhist conception of Emptiness here, much as he does with the other chapters of Five Rings—in the Buddhist conception of the Void, emptiness does not imply that something is missing. Rather, the Void can be that which we conceptually understand to exist in the universe or "out there" and can feel, but can't necessarily see physically.

My intention with the Book of Emptiness is to leave it open ended so that we as the bboy community can continue to discuss things that are relevant to our culture. In this version of *The Book of Five Cyphers* I've included pieces written by other dancers that have something wonderful to say, and a perspective different from my own—it is because of this different perspective that I so value their opinions and believe that you can grow from reading what they have to say.

The Book of Emptiness will remain on open discussion in later editions of this book and through The Book of Five Cyphers website.

Continue to walk your Path.

– Y-Roc

A WHACKO'S JOURNEY

At 13 yrs. old   I danced for the first time in the school talent show.

At 17 yrs. old   I battled for the first time at Cellspace and almost quit the same night.

5-6 yrs.   I didn't touch the floor due to a wrist injury.

At 23 yrs. old   I questioned whether or not I was a bboy.

At 25 yrs. old   I spoke with Trac 2 and got the definition of what a bboy is.

At 26 yrs. old   I got serious and more confident with my dance.

2008- 2012   I shook the world winning competitions and establishing my name in.

2013   I broke my foot and lost that confidence I once had.

2014   I organized the last Cellspace jam and understood what community is.

2015   I set out a goal to win both Renegades 32nd anniversary and Freestyle Session's first ever Rock Dance competition. It was a struggle as I hadn't competed in 2yrs since my injury, a humbling experience relearning how to battle, and lastly joyous achieving both of my goals.

Never question the why because the why will kill you.
-Lemmie Hill (my grandfather)

INSIDE THE MIND OF RAWSKELETON: A DIFFERENT PERSPECTIVE

I go by Rawskeleton of the worldwide known b-boy crew The Freakshow. We created and are recognized for a style that we formed throughout time. I knew when I connected with The Freakshow in 2004 that we we're about to emerge with all the like minded energy surfacing. Our inspiration has always been eclectic music of different genres, Cirque Du Soliel, and martial arts.

We fought endlessly to gain our respect in the b-boy scene. Always thriving on being oneself, staying original and never following the norm. Our motto has always been think outside the box. Expand our minds and push our bodies limits.

Everyone strives to be great but we created an energy that would impact generations to come. We're freaks, we always challenge each other to go far and beyond, do the unbelievable and impossible.

We never thought our movement would grow and inspire across the globe but, throughout time as the art developed we started to get positive feedback and the younger generation as well as older has shown tremendous love and respect.

My mind has always been outside of the box. I like to expand my mind in different types of art forms such as; poetry, fine art/graffiti art, fashion, music, and practice a healthy lifestyle. I'm a self taught yogi and I believe firmly in being true to thyself. It's very important that I never forget where I came from and continue being proud of what I represent. My image as well as my crew has always been to keep a raw mentality and be aggressive. Never follow, always lead.

Over time we all grow and transform trying to find oneself, it's the journey of an artist you live for. To get lost and then find yourself, experiment, take risk, and never be afraid to take chances. Have no regrets, be a part of the change. Spread the Freakquency! We all have unique minds, but it's how we use them for our greater being. When I create and dance I lose myself and tune out. I'm no longer here or there, just an organism. I think of weird shapes and how can you construct your body with movement and momentum to flow effortlessly with precision staying consistent and always creating.

BUILDING COMMUNITY
FOR THE NEXT GENERATION

-KEN MASTERS OF THE FREAK SHOW

Originally I wanted to write about myself and my experiences, but the thing I can't get away from is the fact that there is a certain essence missing. I've been across the U.S. and seen a number of scenes dying. I've also seen that we have the power to bring life back.

We need to pass our knowledge to the next generation. We need to teach kids about the culture. We need individuals to be leaders.

WHY ARE OUR SCENES DYING?

There are two reasons.

1. People don't do it for the love.
2. There's always an "in-crowd" in the scenes that keep some people in, and push other people down.

Personally, I know what it feels like to be hopeless in my life, and I turned to the dance as a way to escape. I never thought that the negativity that I was trying to escape from in my personal life would also exist in the Hip Hop world. I loved bboying though, and fought through the negativity. There are plenty of kids that find Hip Hop because it's so positive, but end up quitting because there are negative people in the scene.

People also make the mistake of trying to grow into a super dancer in the ideal dream of "making it." If you're always winning jams in your scene, that's great, but if you crush the hope out of people, you'll have no one to exchange with—there will be no scene.

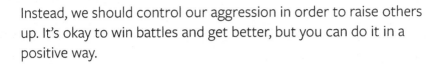

Instead, we should control our aggression in order to raise others up. It's okay to win battles and get better, but you can do it in a positive way.

HOW CAN WE MAKE OUR SCENES A POSITIVE PLACE?

It's important to preserve the culture and keep it true to the essence, but to fix our current problem, people need to take a step down and let their ego go. It's killing the scene. Especially those who are leading the scene. They need to build up the next generation and stop with the negativity.

It takes a lot of time to become a pro bboy and the people that get there are super dope. To be honest though, we were all wack at one point. It's because we were wack that we understand where kids who start are coming from. We're in a position where we should show love and pass it down. Those kids are the ones who will be the leaders of Hip Hop in the future.

HOW CAN WE BUILD UP THE NEXT GEN?

There are OGs and experienced bboys that are in a position to do this. Take the UDEF and non-UDEF jams. There should always be both these types of options, and the prizes that you win at some jams will be different than at the other. The love you get at one jam will be different than at the other. We need to focus on a way that people can relate to one another and get beyond the struggle. We can do this anywhere.

No one should feel turned down. We will do a lot better for the community by building people up.

HOW CAN WE KEEP
THE STATE OF BBOYING HEALTHY?

It starts with talking to each other. Some might think what we do is crazy. There are many that won't understand why we do this. When you've seen cities burned down, crooked cops, prostitutes on street corners...when you've been in that, people WANT to see art. They want to escape from reality. Don't take it for granted. That's why we do this.

People talk about how bboying and our art form is about love and unity. Somewhere along the line though, it stopped being about that for some people. Instead of starting wars, this should be someplace you can go that's positive, a place you can get involved.

It's a different perspective that people don't see, but if you start from there, everything will work itself out.

WHAT ABOUT
THE STATE OF BBOYING NOW?

The state of this art is not as dope as it's made out to be, and there is a lot of negativity in it. People talk about what will help the community, but (without calling anyone out) there are often things behind the scenes that we don't always see going on. Do people ask questions about it? No. If we continue to accept things as they are, no one will ever get a chance.

It's like most of us are being double out-casted. In our real lives people don't understand us, so we turn to art. But then we're shunned in this community too. This should be a culture where we're accepted for what we are. No matter what you do (art, martial arts, anything!), you should start from a place of respect for people and who they are. We're in a culture where people should love us for who we are.

FIGHT THE GOOD FIGHT.

I'm down to fight for this cause. The scene needs love and passion, we don't need dope dancers. It's the ones who love it and respect each other that will ultimately bring a scene up. When you're fighting for a good cause and something that isn't yourself...while it might not work out right away, when you build others up, people will see it.

I've had judges come up to me and say to my face "sorry man, but I didn't vote for you. I voted for my boy," or "you battle my student, and if you don't have any rep, I won't vote for you." Hip Hop is broken, and it won't be fixed until we can give up our egos. Battling should be a learning experience that brings others (and ourselves) up. We shouldn't seek to destroy others in the process.

We need to teach and support each other on and off the dance floor. Remember, if you're a bboy, you might be someone's hero. Like Poe One says "It's a life battle—always." We can learn to cope with this through the dance, and how to be better people. It doesn't even have to be Hip Hop or art in general, just something you love doing. Seems like we've lost track of that though.

The more I do this and the more I'm it in, I start to realize what was important...it wasn't the dance, it wasn't the battles, it was the people.

A LOOK AT THE 808 BREAKERS: CREW AND FAMILY

-ARK OF THE 808 BREAKERS

Out of respect to our history, I'll give you the long, explicit version of it—it's a lot more like the entire story of our crew, as members have come and gone, and the crew has literally snowballed into what it is today.

Our iteration of the 808 Breakers is, in fact, the 3rd generation of the crew. In 2005 a group of solo bboys in Hawaii came together with the purpose to win competitions. The leader, Justice, had recently moved to the islands and was a part of the LA Breakers— hence the name, "808 Breakers" was chosen for the assembled "super crew." At the time, they were some of the best in the islands and succeeded in making their name known for a short amount of time and even went on to battle names such as "Rock Steady Crew" and "Massive Monkees." Similar to the story of most crews, members of the original 808 Breakers moved on and away from breaking all together in order to take care of and pursue interests in matters concerning family, kids, jobs, among other things.

Justice left the islands in the late 2000's and put the crew's title in the hands of Solid who began to represent the name in 2007 with a squad of two other solo bboys for the next 2 years. Due to personal conflicts, both individuals ended up leaving the crew in 2008.

Towards the end of 2008 I had begun dancing and was trying to find every possible way to dance. I went down the street from my house with the cardboard from a soda box to practice headspins over dog-shit ridden grass. Unbeknownst to me, a guy named Jared (who would end up joining the crew and become one of my best friends) happened to live next to the park and decided to introduce himself to me and explain to me that there was a local call-out battle that happened over Myspace that would be taking place at a nearby rec-center the following day.

Being shocked to hear that there were even bboys living in my neighborhood, I made my way to the rec-center and met the small handful of local bboys from my town (Kaneohe) who were battling a handful of bboys from across the mountains (Pauoa/Honolulu). It was nerve-racking to meet so many kids for the first time all at once, but after six hours of battling and goofing off, we crammed 9 people into a small civic and found the presence to enjoy Jack-in-the-box together. As time went on, I got closer with the bboys from my side of the island (Red, Pathos, Pogo) and would keep in touch with the bboys from the "other side" (Attack, Dream, Shoyu).

Moving towards college and making a small degree of success initially as a solo bboy in the scene, I was confronted by Solid and brought to the University of Hawaii's practice spot as a prospect for a new generation of 808 Breakers. Bringing all of my neighborhood friends, I came to the meeting and was met with none other than the guys we had battled several months prior! The chemistry we all had together was immediate.

From 2008-2011 we succeeded as a crew in filing as an LLC. (808 Breakers LLC.), became sponsored by several clothing brands, and performed over a hundred times in the span of 3 years. We were featured in local music videos, commercials, participated in television interviews, and gave speeches at schools' anti-drug rallies with DARE. All the while, competitively being overshadowed by local crews such as Red Eyed Jedis and ABC Crew. We were young, impressionable kids with a drive for something greater. During this time, we welcomed five members into our squad, two of which are still active (Funky T/Tyler Tuiasosopo, and Oolong-D/David Harada)

In 2011 our crew hit rough waters as deep personal complications between members hit an all-time high that resulted in physical and verbal disputes as a result of drug-use, drug-dealing, and situations regarding girlfriends. As a result, our previous leader, Solid, left the crew as well as one of my neighborhood best friends, Pathos. During this time, a number of other members either left or stopped breaking all-together.

Between 2011-2012 I became the default leader of the crew as I was already in charge of many things regarding the organization of our business/performances and had the drive to continue battling. At the beginning of this time, there were three of us representing at battles (often, full crew battles) for the sake of fun and enjoyment of the dance. Though things were chaotic in terms of personal relationships with previous members as well as the general "growing pains" that every person in their early 20's goes through, we held together and continued to perform and battle. During these two years we welcomed Hijack (Jack Rabanal) and Arctic Fox (Jordan Rull) into our crew. Although we continued to lose the vast majority of battles we entered locally, we put every single penny that we earned (as well as personal savings) into buying flights for ourselves to represent at jams such as Evolution (2010), Massive Monkees Day, and Freestyle Session.

During 2012, things began to fall together as our first crew victory was a Freestyle Session Qualifier in Hawaii. A few of our members were looking at graduating from college and moving back to the continental US and saw the opportunity to represent as a family so we flew literally every one of our members to LA. Ayo (Adam) had been around for our performances during this time and generally getting along with all of us in the parties we found ourselves in, joined the crew.

College ended for myself and I moved to San Francisco at the start of 2013 where I went through my own personal journey that was largely centered around breaking. The crew represented in the islands and got around to seeing new members including the Kung Jew (Boaz) and Kid Karma (Alex) join our crew. I went through a rocky divorce and initially flew Hijack to San Francisco to live with me and help manage the classes I was teaching. As the months went on, we decided to bring Karma to the mix as he was young, available, and willing to make the leap. We essentially lived in a studio apartment the size of a garage, which, for three young guys, was not easy—but definitely developed us together as crew members. In a relatively short amount of time, we represented all over the country battling both local and international crews alike.

As we go forward into this new time, both Karma and Hijack will move back to Hawaii to contribute to the rebuilding of the local scene. A vast majority of our members are spread between places such as Seattle, San Diego, and New Jersey. We will continue to represent globally and have plans to begin throwing events in the islands that will focus on bringing people together within the islands as well as provide an outlet for "outside" bboys to come to experience the islands.

ON CREW CHEMISTRY

Our crew has built their chemistry on personal relationships with each other that are practically independent of the dance itself. While we make it a point to train and practice together, our primary focus of being a crew is staying connected with each other's lives—whether it be through sharing disgusting memes, or making crude jokes about each other's body parts. All of our members have gone through a range of personal trials outside of dance and have had our collective crew "be there" for them during that time. It is somewhat ironic, that the chemistry of our dance crew has very little to do with dance and much more to do with spending meaningful time doing completely meaningless and slightly moronic activities with each other.

Not all friendships, relationships, or crews are meant to be—and this is OKAY. In the same way that you can be friendly to someone, but you can't force a friendship with him/her—you can practice/battle together with a group of people (forever, maybe), but doing so will have NO impact on your desire to dance with them and stick with them, regardless of their performance. When it comes to it, true chemistry is not something that is "built," or "created," from nothing, it is something that can only be expanded on naturally through time and (usually) trials. Chemistry can be "tested," however, and the best way to do so is to simply spend time with members outside of the dance floor.

ON BATTLING AS A CREW

As far as battling together as a crew, having every member locked onto the same mentality is essential to the delivery of a message or strategy when the moment calls. Communicating with each other during and before the jam is critical. At times, certain battles call for being calm, collected, and thoughtful, while others call for wild, unbridled, risk-taking. Though it's never completely in one person's control, it's important to have all members together with the overall frequency that the crew possesses.

There are limitless ways to stay present and engaged, as a group however, most will reveal themselves if you tend to physically bring all members together in the minutes PRIOR to the battle.

I feel like most of our energy comes from the fact that we've felt like underdogs for all of our lives. As a crew, we've felt "backed into a corner" at nearly every single jam since our conception in this dance and constantly return to the attitude that each battle could be or last. We have grown, both as individuals, and as a family through constantly pushing ourselves in this mindset against opponents that we never could have imagined battling.

I might also add that we all maintain perspective when it comes to battling—that is to say that, we take what we do seriously in our own personal performance, but not seriously to an identity-shattering extent. This effectively "frees" us to behave however we please. There really is no rhyme or reason to anything we do prior or after a jam—we've partied, skated, argued, fought, gotten arrested, eaten inordinate amounts of awful fast-food, played street fighter—the only rule is that we do it together.

ON CREWNITY

All crews are not made of dancers, they are made of people. At the end of the day, if the only reason why you're battling with some other person is to win a competition or gain notoriety, then you're missing the point of what a crew is all together. Personally, I notice the "realest" moments of being with my crew are those that make me enjoy what I'm doing with my time and energy.

Not every crew is formed with the same purpose or even maintains the same dynamic. Some crews are together to win competitions, some are together because of family, some are together because they share the same artistic ideas towards the dance—all crews that are successful in their journey know and are honest about why they are together. These things change and have everything to do with the growth of personalities than ability. Maintaining and growing together as a crew is about individually being willing to accept and explore relationships, both internal and external, through the tests that life throws you.

THOUGHTS ON
STYLE AND INFLUENCE

-SUMO OF ROCK SO FRESH

HOW DID YOU INNOVATE YOUR STYLE?

I honestly just had an obsession with trying to represent the epitome of what a bboy should look like. I went off of my main influences at the time. The movies Style Wars and The Freshest Kids. Also Rock So Fresh, The Get Right Gang (Joey Gold), Flow Master, music from the Super Bbeat Boys, and my crew at the time Lil Wizards.

I was always motivated by just trying to make my teachers proud and wanted them to KNOW they were passing on their thoughts and beliefs mentally and physically on to me in the truest form.

WHAT ELSE ARE YOU INFLUENCED BY?

As far as developing my foundation...foundation is 50 percent of how good something is going to look. The other half is what you are influenced by. I've only done a few things in my life that I've taken pretty serious that will always influence me in the way I think. I played basketball, skateboarded, and I still dance. I have a lot of skateboarding influences but mainly Daewon Song. My big brother and I always looked up to him and the speed, power, and technicality he had. We skated that way and I take the same approach to my breaking.

HOW DO YOU TO KEEP PUSHING THE LIMITS OF A STYLE CONSIDERED BY MANY AS "TRADITIONAL??

As far as pushing limits...it's just trying to keep things fun and new. I don't look at my dancing like its traditional...it's just me, I don't have a choice. So anything I do that's "new" is going to have that traditional flair to it because that's my foundation and I wouldn't have it any other way.

WHAT KEEPS YOU GOING?

I've been dancing since I was 16. That's 13 years ago. (Fuck.) I've always danced because it makes me happy and I take pride in what I do on the floor.

That's what drives me...I can go for a long time with that one but that's it.

FINDING YOUR
INDIVIDUAL DIRECTION

-EDDIE STYLES OF ROCK SO FRESH

ON COMMON PITFALLS FOR BBOYS/BGIRLS

Approaching the dance with the wrong mentality happens a lot in our bboy scene. Some of the pitfalls that boys tend to fall into are like dancing because of money. Yes it could be a source of income when done professionally but going into it because that's all that matters and you want to make a quick buck ruins the actual integrity of this dance. This shouldn't be in anyone's mind yet! More important is developing your skills and finding out why you love to bboy would be first. You also don't really get to enjoy the dance due to always worrying about when the next jam is to make ends meet.

Another pitfall would be not really understanding our culture. Bboying is the first dance of Hip Hop so taking the right steps to learn the history/development and knowledge of bboying and further more Hip Hop in general, gives you a better look on how to approach the dance. We have so many resources nowadays that it should not be an excuse that there isn't enough information to be educated on bboying.

Last that I would warn boys would be the fake approach...YUP! STOP BEING FAKE!! One thing that everyone really dislikes is bboys that think they are thugs or hard asses and after a battle or off the floor you are super nice and want to go drink boba after. Shit don't work that way, you act like an ass in a battle then you better be an ass outside as well. You lose respect and credibility. Just be yourself and really embrace the fact that you have the ability and gift to dance. Don't act tough if you ain't tough. Now if you are? Then good for you. Some are that way due to rough upbringings or just had a crazy life. Just don't fake the funk.

ON INNOVATING YOUR STYLE

Rock So Fresh has been around for 15 years now. We have always carried the traditional essence of bboying throughout the years with the way we think, dress and dance. At the time RSF was created we wanted to be different due to the scene being stagnant and all looking the same. We wanted to take a different direction and focus on what inspired us when we danced. Personally for me it was the Original Rock Steady Crew and New York City Breakers. We all have our own ideas and inspirations but we all have the same train of thought. With that being said we consistently keep pushing ourselves to innovate and keep up with what's relevant due to being open minded and excepting that this dance evolves. By staying true to our own beliefs and traditional foundation we can still evolve and keep things fresh by adding new grooves, moves and nuances to what we have and learn on a daily basis. We also grow and share together with our crew. I feel like this is important for many that are in crews. You must share and grow together to build a trust-bond with each other to push and motivated one another. Making things fresh is key to what we do in our crew. And believe me when I say it takes time to develop that certain confidence to know when you are fresh with your movement and style.

ON BUILDING INNOVATIVE FLOWS AND COMBOS, AND THE THEORY OF "NEGATIVE SPACE"

-M-PACT OF UNDERGROUND FLOW

I believe there is a balance that we need to understand as a B-boy/B-girl when it comes to building effective combos. The combos we create whether it's great or horrible can be effective depending on how the move is performed and expressed. I like say, "it's how you do it, and not the moves you choose to use." This is where style comes to play and for a beginner, this lesson may take years to understand and discover. For instance, a B-boy can perform with a 200% confident attitude with the intent to rock a footwork pattern into a leg thread transition to a freeze on the beat, and this can have the same result as another B-boy performing 2 one-handed airflares. The moves we choose to perform don't always give us the same impact we want when we perform it with no intention. It is important to have intention in your movements with your unique style.

Once our intention becomes second nature through our movements, our stylistic combos can become more powerful than the moves itself. However, the moves you choose to perform can also create the level of impact of your combos as well. For example, if you choose to do one airflare to two rounds of 1990s while threading your leg into an airchair, the result of this combo will most likely make the crowd go wild and scream, and likely get you good marks from the judges. This is why there is a balance and importance to understanding your movements and movement intentions.

A good b-boy/b-girl will create effective moves within a combo to surprise the crowd and judges while a great b-boy/b-girl will create stylistic combos with an intention to execute his or her opponent. An overall b-boy/b-girl should understand this balance and apply both understandings to create the most effective combos and make any situation in his or her favor.

When it comes to finding inspirations to build effective combos, my brother VilIN and I like to think of a saying that we tell each other, "If it's easy than it's already been done." It's the level of difficulty or creativity that is applied to the unique combos that makes it fun or exciting to watch. I get inspired each time I challenge myself to create hard combos that I know someone will likely not be able to replicate or perform. Another way I find inspiration to build combos or moves is to simply let go and free my mind to allow myself to make mistakes. When you choose to honestly believe in your natural movements and freestyle, you will discover some of your most essential combos and signature moves by mistake. Again, this is another lesson that can be hard for beginners to grasp, but once it's understood, another world of creativity opens.

Once you believe that there are no wrongful mistakes in creating, you will never make an error that is not beneficial to you as b-boy/b-girl. I believe there will always be different methods to innovate and create new moves from of old moves, and even to create moves that's never been seen or done. This idea of the creative process being infinite and divine inspires and urges me to continue to build and grow as a unique B-boy. There is no end point, and I believe somehow, we are all looking deep inside ourselves to find a point of ending satisfaction. With no ego, we will see that we are all a student in this culture, and there are no true master b-boys/b-girls. We only seek to be masters in own mind and is constantly battling ourselves to become a master that we choose and want to be, and this is why I get inspired to create myself as a b-boy. I love battling myself and learning from the B-boy that I am.

ON NEGATIVE SPACE

There are many methods that I use to build moves and flows. One that I would like to share is the concept of holes and negative space. This is harder to explain through writing compared to showing in person. However, the point of this creative concept is to use your negative space and the variety of open holes to help you create new transitions, threads, flows, moves and so on. For example, when squatting in footwork position, you will notice many pathways through negative space and one hole between both feet that are open for you to move and weave through. Once you place one hand down to the floor to close in on a negative space, this opens new holes to initiate new potential pathways. If you understand and see this, you can then slowly apply certain movements to create flows and moves that you might have never experimented with in certain positions. This is also a great way to train to get out of awkward positions that we all tend to find ourselves in when we are cyphering or battling.

THE BEAUTY
OF
MOVEMENT

"My mother showed me the beauty of movement. At family parties I gazed as her hips swayed to salsa music with an infectious electricity that lit up the dance floor. I watched as the room danced together, liberated from life's stresses, pulsating in unison to the heartbeat of a song. It was in that moment that my relationship with movement began. I have come to understand how movement is a gift. I have experienced the ways in which the ability to move can enhance a person's life, and how the inability to move can stifle it. As a dancer who has struggled to find ways to continue moving while facing chronic injuries, I have felt the immense pain of loss and the joy of self-discovery. Each obstacle I have overcome has been an opportunity to grow in my capacity to heal, teach and support others facing adversity. Two years ago, while getting treated for an ACL tear my doctor found that I needed surgery in both of my hips. I was told that my hip anatomy predisposed me to cartilage damage, and my physical activity growing up had exacerbated the problem. Though initially discouraged by injuries to continue dancing, I remembered the beauty of breaking. Dancers are not limited to using their legs to dance; our heads, backs and extremities are canvases by which to paint masterpieces. I knew I could find safe new ways to dance that did not strain my hips. These challenges only strengthened my commitment to find new ways to move and my drive to continue dancing. Losing my ability to move one way to set me free in more ways than I thought imaginable. I continue to search for innovative ways to safely express myself in this craft. I have used these challenges as learning opportunities to support others to a greater capacity. Thank you to this dance for giving me this medium to unlock my full potential."

– Francis Tongpalad

ABOUT THE AUTHOR

Cory "Y-Roc" Howell is co-founder of Uncomfortably Fresh Crew and a resident of San Diego. After watching Li Yi Min's "Drunken Arts, Crippled Fist," he started trying backflips in the dirt in his front yard. A serendipitous find of The Freshest Kids at Lou's Records in Encinitas put him on his current Path.

Y-Roc works as an accountant at a San Diego based educational not-for-profit and spends eight hours a day hoping that by crunching numbers, he's helping get kids to college. He writes fiction and douchey poetry on napkins and yellow notepads. He likes drawing pictures of Emiliano Zapata, trees, and people he sees at coffee shops.

Questions, comments, or interested in submitting to future projects? Contact us at fivecyphers@gmail.com

CPSIA information can be obtained
at www.ICGtesting.com
Printed in the USA
FSOW04n0217220616
21839FS